A STRUM + BANG
Literary Drift

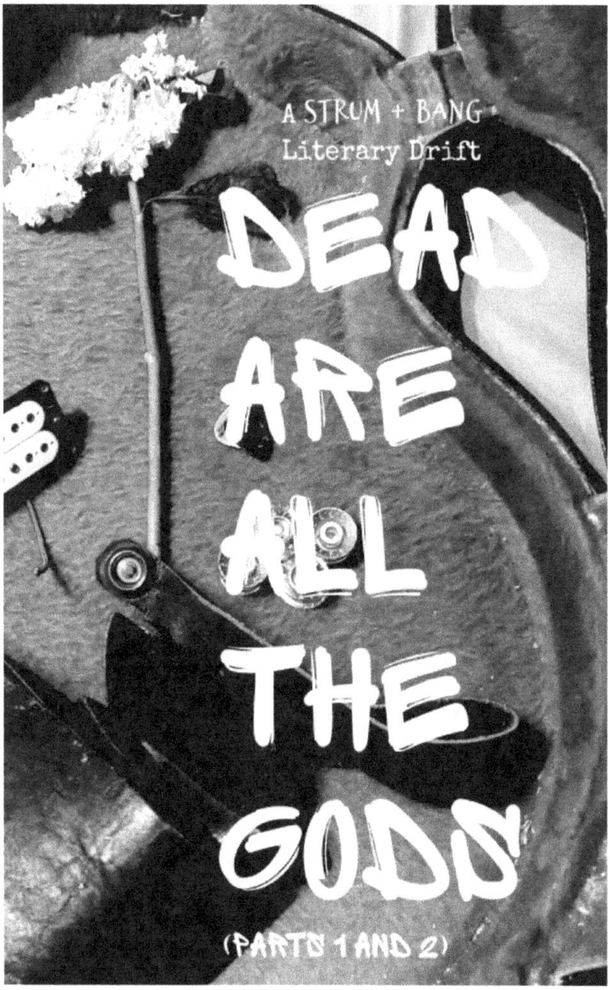

DEAD ARE ALL THE GODS

(PARTS 1 AND 2)

Cover Art by Strum + Bang

Illustrations by Jaclyn McKay

www.jaclynmckay.com

ISBN: 9798870095141

For Camille,
the true music in my life
and

Jaclyn and Jessica,
the original Melody and Harmony

<u>In Memoriam:</u>

Kevin F. - the voice that gave life to the music

Richie Corona - a FLIGHT O.G. and true Bronx original

Mark Hitt - Legend.

If I were not a physicist, I would probably be a musician.
- Albert Einstein

You just pick up a chord, go twang, and you've got music.
- Sid Vicious

Contents

Author's Note

So if all these essays, posts, or whatever they are have already been published on-line, why put them into print? Well, my editor felt it would be a good idea to revisit them, correct some of the glaring grammar and spelling issues (which I blame mostly on auto-correct trying to make me look bad), see if my opinions have changed (organically or by lawsuit), and to meet my contractual obligation for a final book, kinda like how Prince's *Chaos and Disorder* album was released to get Warner Bros off his back (this was the whole changing his name to a symbol while writing "Slave" on his face era).

Okay, so now that all the preceding responsibly-presented jargon is out of the way...none of what I just said is completely true (except for the Prince part, and the grammar and spelling part, and the editor part...hmmm, maybe none of it was true). I put this book together just because I wanted to do it. Books are simply cooler than posts.

Oh, and I am my own editor (more on that coming up), which explains all the grammar and spelling issues in the first place...but, quoted statements are presented exactly as they were offered, so if the guy from Greta Van Fleet failed high school English take it up with the Michigan school system...and if you still find errors...well, you probably got this book for free anyway, so fuck off. It's a fun book, not a thesis.

So enjoy your (probably free) book, ponder the ideas presented (as silly as they may seem, true consideration was given to the subjects), have a thought and/or a chuckle, and keep your nitpicks and grammar-policing to yourself. I'm sure even Hemingway had his finger-waggers and tsk-tsk-ers. (Yes, I just compared myself to Hemingway. Write your own book and you can compare yourself to whoever you want...well, maybe not that Greta Van Fleet guy.)

Editor's Note

So, yep, still me…(editors cost money). In the time si nce these essays, posts, or whatever they are were "published," some of the reference points have changed. Neil Peart has passed (tragic), Jeff Beck has also passed (very sad), with his last performance being one with Johnny Depp (even sadder), Amber Heard allegedly pooped on Johnny Depp's pillow (unrelated to the book but still hilarious), Jeremy Renner ran himself over with a snow plow (and miraculously lived to tell the tale), William Shatner actually went into space (and hated it!), Charlie Watts passed (no reports of Keith Richards snorting his ashes as he did with his own father's…really), and Taylor Swift's *Eras* concert tour had a measurable impact on the GDP of the United States while her screaming fans triggered an actual seismic event in Seattle (the birthplace of Jimi Hendrix…the irony of which you will understand once you read the first essay). Like I said, genuine thought was mustered (often painfully) to give meaningful, fun, and thought-provoking insights into these topics and the people mentioned within. Musicians and the gifts they share can do amazing things for us all. Even if some of these essays don't relate to your specific musical or cultural tastes, read them with an open mind and try to find the common thread that links us all through music. There's a reason we still listen to the music of the past as if it was brand new, and new music as if it was a promise for the future. It transports us, it transforms us, and it unites us. To paraphrase that apocryphal quote, it's called "Classic" rock for a reason. Hopefully you will be reminded of a song you forgot about, decide to rethink your opinion of a particular artist, or take a chance on something you never heard before.

Either way…Rock on.

The Werks

The following essays were originally published on

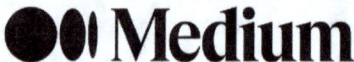

between December of 2018 and March of 2021

under the publication

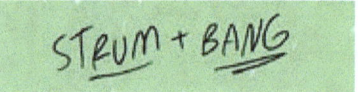

Originally Published Dec 27, 2018

Dead Are All the Gods (Part One)

Part 1: Is Taylor Swift the new Jimi Hendrix?

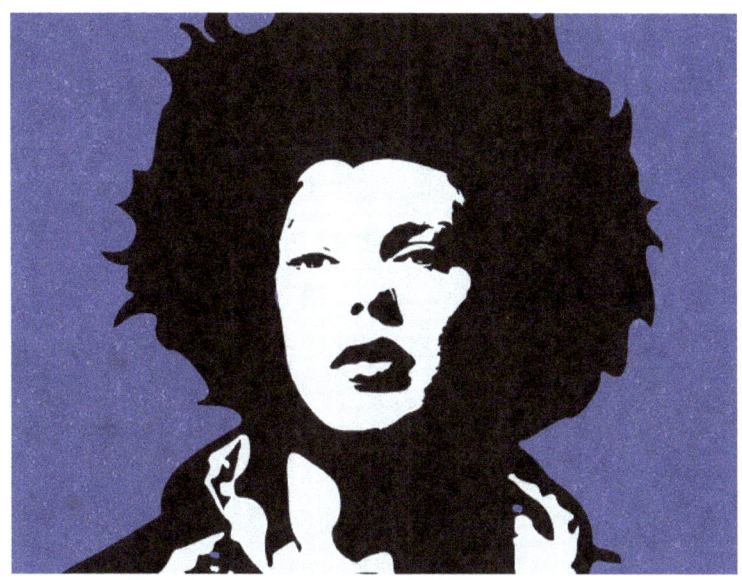

Though "God is dead!" is what we appropriate from the deep, intense, potentially dangerous and utterly blasphemous (insert sarcastic smirk) rhetoric of the lifetime's work of Nietzsche, Mainlander, Hegel, Heidegger and all those other morose German philosophers, there is another quote in Thus Spoke Zarathustra — "Dead are all the gods…" that comes into play for the theme of this article: Loud guitars — and the equally loud, proud, unapologetic and awe-inspiring players (i.e., the gods) who wield them (past and present).

Geoff Edgers wrote an article for the Washington Post back in 2017 called, "Why My Guitar Gently Weeps — The slow, secret death of the six-string electric, and why you should care." I feel that there are two quotes in the piece that are revelatory. One is from George Gruhn, the well-known guitar expert who has sold instruments to every significant player to ever pass through Nashville. He said of the premise of the dying electric, "What we need is guitar heroes… Eric Clapton is my age." (Gruhn was 71 at the time of the article.) He drove that point home by adding, "You don't see a bunch of kids emulating John Mayer and listening to him and wanting to pick up a guitar because of him."

The second, more disturbing, quote in that WAPO article is from Andy Mooney, Fender's CEO, who states that Taylor Swift is "the most influential guitarist of recent years."

Chew on that for a minute…and away we go.

In the mid-60s, some excitable boy in London spray-painted the phrase "Clapton is God" in the underground station in Islington (that translates to "the subway" for us non-tea drinkers here in NYC).

Clapton had apparently impressed some youngsters with his guitar playing in John Mayall and the Bluesbreakers (a band he would royally screw by walking away in the middle of a tour after royally screwing the Yardbirds by walking away just

3

as they started to break big in order to join the Bluesbreakers). Whether you agree or disagree with their sentiment, it was the start (kind of) of a very realized idea of the guitar-slinging god of rock. There were already big rock stars like Elvis and the Beatles on the scene, but a singular idol based solely around the guitar was a fresh fetish. Comparing musicians to God was particularly offensive and disrespectful to the establishment (remember the "more popular than Jesus Christ" comment that John Lennon made that caused Beatles records to be burned across America — crazy shit right there), but like anything that rattles the older folks, this movement was now up and running.

A very real argument can be made that black musicians were once again out ahead of this trend in music. Obviously, Charlie Christian and Robert Johnson were long regarded as legendary, and if anybody was a guitar-slinging original it was Chuck Berry. He did it all: he could play — he invented guitar licks that are still being used to this day (Johnny Be Goode, anyone?); he owned the stage — his duck walk is instantly recognizable (and would soon be appropriated, along with many of his riffs, by the upcoming guitar gods); he could write and he could sing. Chuck Berry falls into that time in music history when America was afraid of black performers influencing their children. Just look at Chuck's and even Little

Richard's career. As unique and talented as they were, their music had to be re-routed and re-packaged to the American audience through the British Invasion bands.

So, while Clapton may have had his moment in the sun, the new guitar god imagery was already about to get blown up for real by a dude from Seattle (and in no small irony after the Chuck Berry discussion, this dude was black).

Jimi Hendrix was the real deal. There were obviously some of the greatest to ever play guitar around at the time like Beck, Page, Townshend and company, but when Hendrix went to London in September of 1966, the game changed forever. The guy could play like no other, but it was his physical relationship with the guitar that was stunning. Pete Townshend was alleged to be the most pissed off by Hendrix and his stage style, and Clapton was said to be less than thrilled about Hendrix's absolute mastery of the instrument. Hendrix's Monterey and Woodstock performances cemented his evergreen status as the quintessential guitar god, as well as making people take a different look at the Fender Stratocaster, which up until that point had been primarily viewed as the guitar Buddy Holly made famous.

Playing at Woodstock with a right-handed Strat turned upside-down (1968 Fender Stratocaster, Serial №240981, Olympic White — which Paul Allen bought in 1993 for 1.3

million), opening people's eyes and ears to the tremolo bar (Holy shit! That's what that's for!), and all this against the backdrop of those beautiful Marshall stacks.

Hendrix may have single-handedly given Fender the level of credibility it still holds as a premier rock guitar. When Hendrix died, there was a void that the guitar disciples may have seen as unfillable, but there was an upcoming guy who seemed ready to bring it to the next level — Jimmy Page.

Jimmy Page was quietly waiting in Clapton's wake. Page was an emerging studio guy who ended up with the slot in the Yardbirds — along with Beck — after Clapton's exit. As a Yardbird, Page was somewhat unremarkable. He was kinda just back there, almost second fiddle to Beck, who unquestionably made the most out of his time with the band. It was after the breakup of that band that things changed. Page had been playing a Telecaster that Jeff Beck gave him (which Fender is issuing as a signature model soon in both the initial "mirror" design and the subsequent hand painted dragon version), and he brought that guitar with him to his next project — the New Yardbirds (a name mercifully discarded thanks to John Entwistle).

With the release of *Led Zeppelin*, rock guitar skulduggery would never be the same. Page had been tinkering with a violin bow on some live shows, but now it was on vinyl.

"Dazed and Confused" was a true WTF! moment for guitar playing wannabes everywhere. Then the stars aligned, and Joe Walsh (of all people) helped define the image of a guitar god forever. In 1969, after seeing Led Zeppelin live, Joe Walsh decided that Page needed a Les Paul (though he had previously played a 1960 Black Beauty Custom with a Bigsby that was stolen at an airport), and he hand-delivered the guitar that would come to define a generation—Page's "Number One" : a late 50's Les Paul Standard in a fading sunburst that would come to be desired and imitated to the delight of guitar refinishers across the globe (the guitar had previously been refinished under Walsh's ownership and the original serial number had been removed). Walsh sold it to Page for $1200 (a guitar that could essentially be considered priceless, but undoubtedly would sell for a few million bucks now). Page went on to record "Heartbreaker" with that Les Paul—another seminal moment in guitar goddery (…is that a real word?).

Cut to live Zeppelin shows and people soon forgot about Clapton's moment in the sun of the gods. Here's a lanky dude with a Les Paul hanging ridiculously low, pseudo-duck-walking across the stage (ahem…Chuck Berry); dragon-embroidered silk bell-bottoms and jacket; Marshall Stacks as a backdrop (ahem, ahem… Hendrix); a freaking violin bow; then (just to really blow yer mind), an occasional double-necked Gibson!

Pair him up with the equally god-like prototype for all future front men, the greatest drummer ever and a bass player who does every job on the musical planet, and there it is. The ultimate, quintessential, always imitated, but never duplicated, Mount Olympus of rock and roll — Led Zeppelin — the blueprint for guitar driven, hard and heavy rock music from that moment into eternity.

So, there's the recipe: skinny/lanky dude with somewhat gawky/cool moves on stage; low-hanging guitar (Les Paul preferred, please); some kind of unique stage wear; Marshall Stacks (the more the merrier). Done, end of sentence. Guitar god.

Now, as cool as the low hanging guitar looks, a higher hanging axe has staked a claim too (comfort and access count for something) and was really on display when Eddie Van Halen literally exploded onto the scene in 1978 and the gods had sent forth a new brother. Chest high guitar, finger-tapping haughtiness galore, and metal-plectrum clamped middle finger-and-thumb style oscillating at superhuman velocities. Van Halen needed full access and used every inch of the fretboard. (Hmmm…this could possibly be a Strat thing. Hendrix kept it high; Blackmore kept it high;

Beck keeps it high.) Fender did have a weight advantage over a Les Paul: 7–8 lbs. for a Strat versus 9–11 for an unchambered Les Paul. It makes a big difference when you're playing a long gig, but it was also what made the two guitars sonically unique unto themselves.

Countless others have followed in that vein of guitar goddery (second use — one more and it's officially a word) with one of the most notable being Slash. He came along at the right time. Guns N' Roses took the recipe, mixed in some more guitars (Izzy Stradlin wins the Ron Wood Second Banana award), threw in some onstage moments of rock star excess, and — boom! These guys acted and felt like veteran rockers, which they now are. Slash had the look: hat, hair, shades (he kinda appropriated Slade's Noddy Holder hat thing); he had the chops (smart and melodic leads with just enough testing the boundaries of his blues-laden scale work); he had the sound (excellent tone, awesome sustain, just a really great guitar sound); and the axe — a knock-off Les Paul with a Gibson logo and all! (Uh-oh…part of an emerging issue, though Slash's Kris Derrig guitar may have been far better than the production guitars Gibson was churning out in the 1980s).

From the 60s to the 80s, guitar gods ruled the musical Earth, but now we are left in the ashes of the "most influential guitarist of recent years" quote from the CEO of Clarence Leonidas "Leo" Fender's legacy.

So back to Nietzsche… Here's the full quote: "Dead are all the gods: now we want the overman (uberman) to live." The uberman was Nietzsche's goal for humans to strive towards as creators of new values, and as a solution to the problems of the "death of God". Like George Gruhn said to the Washington Post reporter, we need guitar heroes. And I agree, but pivot a bit. Yes, we do need guitar heroes, but not gods. We need those ubermen who are not so removed from us, but still show us what we can be. Guitar players who we would rather hang out and have a beer with, than put up on a pedestal. When bands like Pearl Jam came along, we got to see what regular dudes making killer music looked like. No crazy costumes, just street clothes, like we wore. The heroes are out there, just look at Dave Grohl. He's like the keeper of the torch. He preserves rock history like no other contemporary artist. He saved the Sound City Neve 8028 soundboard, he recruited Paul McCartney to be the Cobain stand-in at the Nirvana reunion, he inducted RUSH into the Hall of Fame, he even got John Paul Jones back in a band (Them Crooked Vultures), for cryin' out loud. All that and he makes rock history at the same time. His recent gig at MSG was a loud and rowdy guitar driven rock concert like the

Garden hasn't seen in a while. And he does it all with a massive grin like a kid living a dream (which he clearly is). The heroes are out there. There's Zakk Wylde, cranking it out like the journeyman he is (his WYLDE Audio branded guitars are really cool, and sound and play great. He also sees trends — his *Book of Shadows* albums were acoustic-based and excellent). There's someone for everyone. Yes, the giants are still out there, but we also need to spread the love to the wizards: Satriani, Vai, Eric Johnson, Guthrie Govan, Andy Timmons, Greg Howe, Paul Gilbert, Petrucci; the journeymen: Zakk, Luke, Morse, Warren Haynes, Derek Trucks; the blues guys: Kenny Wayne Shepherd, Walter Trout, Coco Montoya, Chris Duarte, Bobby Messano, Philip Sayce, Mato Nanji; the odd dudes: Buckethead, John 5; the multitaskers: Bumblefoot, Richie Kotzen; the future: the Marcus King Band, Jared James Nichols, Gary Clark Jr., Davy Knowles, Black Stone Cherry; the bands who never give up like Dream Theater (BTW, just follow anything Mike Portnoy is involved with: Liquid Tension Experiment, Adrenaline Mob, The Winery Dogs, Sons of Apollo — all great guitar driven music backed by one of the most incredible drummers since Peart); and the blue collar working musicians like Tesla (the two *REAL to REEL* cover albums are great fun for anybody who was in a band in the 80s), The Supersonic Blues Machine, the Dead Daisies; just reach out for any band you

11

like, find them on whatever your platform is, check out related artists and have a go.

Is the electric guitar dead, and have all our gods gone with it? That's really up to us. They obviously aren't going to be around forever, but the music will be. So, show up whenever a guitar is being played, listen to whatever you can, and give something new a try. It's no surprise that Gibson is consolidating its factories into the Nashville plant. Nashville is the epicenter for music now more than ever, and maybe we need to look to the South to save our beloved six string? There are some more than decent country players bordering on rock, like Brad Paisley and Keith Urban (just sayin'...pardner).

So, from all this blabbering, I can deduce a few things for certain—the Les Paul and the Strat are eternal (whether or not the companies survive the apocalypse of their own creation), and there will always be a hero in the making, grabbing a guitar for the first time and thinking 'oh, yeah!'; and NO! Taylor Swift is NOT the new Jimi Hendrix. She's clearly influential, inspirational and motivational for a new generation (not to mention a financial juggernaut), but not in the same way. Not in the guitar way. Not in the "Little Wing" or "Manic Depression" way (not even close). This summer will mark the 50th anniversary of Hendrix's performance of the Star-Spangled Banner at Woodstock. A legendary performance by an iconic guitar master on an iconic guitar. That sound, that image, that historic moment in guitar history will be remembered for another fifty years. Ten years ago, Taylor Swift performed the national anthem at the World Series (no, she did…I'm telling you, it happened…you can look it up…the Phillies won).

Guitar Center may have sold a lot of Baby Taylors (short scale guitars) to Baby Taylors (short scale humans, referred to as "Swifties"), but picking that guitar up will never send chills up your spine and make the hair on your arms stand up the same way that picking up a Fender Stratocaster and feeling the spirit of Jimi Hendrix stir in your soul will. Every…Single…Time.

Rock On.

Originally Published Jan 13, 2019

Run Joe, Run!

Why Joe Walsh just might be the Forrest Gump of Rock and Roll

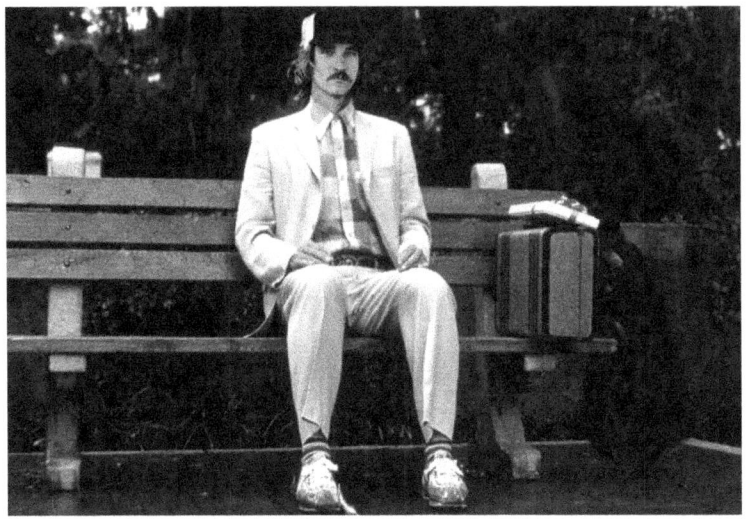

Part of the conceit of 1994's *Forrest Gump* is its insertion of the Tom Hanks character into seemingly random and unconnected events in history which he may or may not have somehow influenced. There's Gump with an unknown Elvis, Gump with JFK, with LBJ, with Nixon, Lennon, Dick Cavett. Though not entirely original (i.e., 1983's *Zelig*), it's a cool concept nonetheless, and it makes you think about people, places and things in a curious light…

So, there I was, listening to Joe Walsh being interviewed about something or another (you can never tell with him…Joe likes to talk), and it just clicked. There's no question

14

Joe Walsh is a truly great guitar player with well thought out licks. Listen to "Life's Been Good", "Rocky Mountain Way" and "Funk 49" a few hundred times (or one weekend on any classic rock station) and you'll start to recognize Joe's signatures. Guitar players know what I'm talking about here. (Not really but go on.) We know all this and think we know Joe, but then this somewhat goofy guy somehow turns up in some truly historic guitar moments that make you say, "wait, what? Joe Walsh was where…and did what…with who? This guy reminds me of someone…but who? (Are you with me here?)

And away we go…

Joe Gump Moment #1: Joe Walsh sold Jimmy Page the 1959 Les Paul (his "Number 1") that would go on to become one of the most influential guitars of all time. The James Gang was sharing the bill with Led Zeppelin on part of their 1969 American tour. Page was playing the "dragon" 1959 Fender Telecaster that Jeff Beck gave him back in the Yardbirds, and a 1960 Black Gibson Les Paul Custom with a Bigsby Tremolo. After killing it as openers on their first go round in America the year before, Zeppelin was back as headliners, but apparently something was still missing, and Joe Walsh knew what it was. Joe told Guitar World back in May 2012, "I laid it on him and said, 'Try this out'. He really liked it, so I gave him a good deal, about $1,200. I had to hand-carry it; plus, I flew there and everything. So whatever my expenses were, that's what I charged him… I just thought he should have a Les Paul, for god's sake!" So, Joe Walsh just thought that Jimmy Page should have that guitar. (Uh-huh.) Nostradamus or Forrest Gump? I'm going Gump. (BTW, it seems that Joe left a couple of good riffs in that axe before he cut it loose. Just sayin'…)

Joe Gump Moment #2: Joe gave Pete Townshend the 1959 Gretsch 6120 guitar and 1959 Fender Bandmaster amp that Pete used on *Who's Next*. Walsh also told Guitar World in that same interview, "I like to give people equipment and stuff. For me, it's a kind of payback. Anyone who is an influence or hero for me, I'm always concerned with how I can balance the karma." OK, so wait a minute here. Walsh is also the guy behind what might be the best non-concept WHO and/or Rock album ever, with some of the greatest power chords in guitar history, including, but not limited to, the absolutely timeless resounding A chord that backs Daltrey's epic primal "YEAH!" as the tune explodes out of Moon's classic drum chaos in "Won't Get Fooled Again"? "Balance the Karma", huh…I'm not buying the Joe Buddha feint. I will always remember that vintage live video with Townshend sliding on his knees through those lasers blasting that chord out on a Les Paul Deluxe. (You just hadda ruin that for me Joe?)

Joe Gump Moment #3: Back when the James Gang played in Nashville, Walsh got friendly with a pedal steel player named Bill West who had come up with a simple version of a "talk box" which he then lent to a fellow pedal steel player, Pete Drake. Drake was brought in by George Harrison to play on the *All Things Must Pass* sessions, which also included an uncredited performance by Peter Frampton on acoustic. Frampton heard Drake using the talk box and was instantly drawn in. This very same device subsequently wound up in the hands of...(wait for it)...Joe Walsh, who used it for the studio cut of "Rocky Mountain Way." This device wasn't powerful enough for live gigs, so Walsh brought it to Bob Heil (pioneering live rock sound system engineer), who came up with a more usable version for live work. (People like Jeff Beck ("She's a Woman") were already tinkering with some version of a talk box, like Kustom Electronics' "The Bag".) A short time later, Peter Frampton's girlfriend called Bob Heil, who knew Frampton from his Humble Pie days, looking for a gift for him. Heil sent the talk box and, well, we know what came next. So, once again, Joe Walsh is there at another pivotal point in guitar history. Accident or intent? Genius or Gump?

Joe Gump Moment #4: By 1975, the Eagles were a hugely successful band. Their *Greatest Hits (1971–1975)* was the biggest selling album of the 20th Century (42 million worldwide) until *Thriller* came along. They had the easy going, half-country, maybe half-rock thing going on, but they hadn't grabbed the attention of hard-core guitar guys just yet. The addition of Don Felder was an improvement, as he is truly a great player (who also owns a 1959 Les Paul and a primo white 1275 double neck—both available as reproductions from the Gibson Custom Shop. Never let a chance for a buck get past over there at Gibson). So, what else could a super successful band need? Well, if you watch the scene in the recent History of the Eagles documentary where they are singing a cappella backstage, their newest member sticks his bandana-covered head in and pops his eyeballs like everyone's crazy uncle singing at the family holiday party, squeezing out that last note. Welcome to the Joe Walsh era of the Eagles. This era did in fact give us one of the greatest dual guitar solos in rock history over the outro of one of the greatest songs in rock history (written by Felder. Fuck you, Don Henley). So now the guitar players are all watching and saying, "hey, that's the Eagles? What else they got?" Well, they got Joe, and one of his finger warm-ups becomes the intro to the closest thing to hard rock they ever did, "Life in the Fast Lane" (fuck you twice, Henley), and the Eagles are suddenly a "rock" band, yet one more album and…BOOM goes the Eagles (Frey and Henley were dicks). Joe was clearly the hapless Gump this time. A live version of "Seven Bridges Road" became their last top 40 hit until Hell froze over, which it did, for all of us. The Eagles decided after 14 years apart that they were only kidding, they didn't break-up, just took a break. Then they set out to break some piggy banks. Their reunion tour ushered in the era of the $100 concert ticket! This was, by most opinions (or at least mine), a money-grabbing power play by Henley, Frey and Irving Azoff, but there in the press conference, photobombing music history again, was our boy Joe. No incidental Gump moment here, though. This one was no accident. (You're often judged by the company you keep, sorry Joe.)

Joe Gump Moment #5: Ringo Starr was recently making the rounds promoting his coffee-table book of photographs "Another Day in the Life". He was on a bunch of shows and programs, but I happened to catch him on Howard Stern's show. Ringo was doing his usual shtick as the luckiest man alive when a few minutes into the interview popped another guest — his very own brother-in-law. This dude is married to Ringo's wife Barbara Bach's sister, Marjorie. This dude was also the first guitarist on Ringo's All-Starr Band tour and has been on just about every tour since, except when needed for his other band - the Eagles! Yes, that dude is our boy, Joe Walsh. Guitarist and bro-in-law to a Beatle (which might make him the second luckiest man alive).

Joe Gump Honorable Mentions: Joe was quite the notable merry prankster in his heyday. He was there when Keith Moon wrecked hotel rooms. Joe says that "One of the most terrifying things that ever happened to me was that Keith Moon decided he liked me." They went on a toilet exploding tear together, literally blowing up hotel toilets. He once spray-painted his jeans with black paint so he and John Belushi could eat at a snooty restaurant that turned them away for wearing blue jeans. Needless to say, they ruined the chairs and were asked not to return. Joe is from Ohio, so is Dave Grohl. Joe contends that he is also an official member of Foo Fighters.

So, in conclusion (far from it, but as far as I want to go with this), life continues to be good so far for our ordinary average guy Joe, and he continues to barnstorm in places only a Gump could. You'll never have to look far to find Joe somewhere in those footnotes about momentous events in Rock and Roll. He's in there, believe me, I checked all night long.

But seriously, folks... Joe Walsh also has a connection to a very tragic event that is reflected upon in Rock history. On

20

May 4, 1970, the Ohio National Guard shot and killed four unarmed students who were protesting Nixon's Cambodian Campaign on the campus of Kent State University. Neil Young wrote the song "Ohio" and CSNY recorded and released it within weeks of the incident. Readers of Rolling Stone picked "Ohio" as the #2 protest song of all time. Among the students at Kent State during that event — Joseph Fidler Walsh. Joe said of the event, "Being at the shootings really affected me profoundly. I decided that maybe I don't need a degree that bad." He left college right after. We're all glad ya did, Joe.

Rock On…

DEAD ARE ALL THE GODS (PARTS 1 AND 2)

Originally Published Feb 7, 2019

The Songs Remain the Same

Is Greta Van Fleet plundering rock classics or saving Classic Rock?

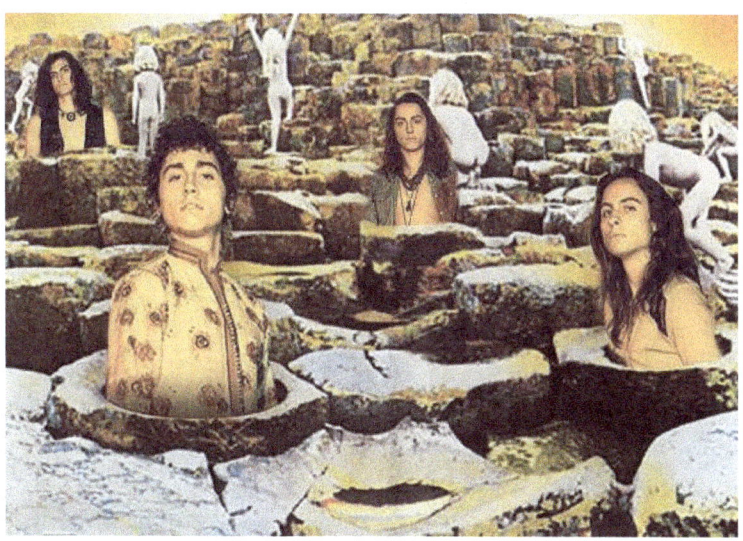

They have already had three №1 songs on Billboard's Mainstream Rock chart. Their first album, *Anthem of the Peaceful Army* (2018), entered the Billboard 200 at №3. Their initial release, *Black Smoke Rising* (2017), was an EP. The second release in 2017 was a double EP called, *From the Fires* (someone needs to explain to me how a "double EP" is different from a regular LP). They are Grammy-nominated for Best Rock Album, Best Rock Song, Best Rock Performance and Best New Artist. They played at Elton

John's private Oscars after-party at his request, and he joined them on stage. They're signed by Lava/Republic and repped by William Morris. They just played on SNL (meh).

To further their pedigree, legendary A&R man Jason Flom personally signed the band (if you're from the New York music scene in the '80s, you know this guy). "Greta Van Fleet is the future of real Rock & Roll," said Flom, now President of Lava Records. "They've got the chops, the swagger and the songs to make their mark as the band of their generation."

These guys are so primed to revive the rock guitar genre, they could even be considered the second coming of...Led Zeppelin?

The first time I ever even heard the name Greta Van Fleet it was coming from the lips of none other than Robert Plant himself! Plant was being interviewed in Australia about his upcoming shows and the interviewer asked about new bands he liked. "There's a band in Detroit called Greta Van Fleet: they are Led Zeppelin I. Beautiful little singer, I hate him! He borrowed it from somebody I know very well!" Wait, what? So, some obscure band from Michigan gets a shout out from Robert Plant!

And their response to this is...

From singer Josh Kiszka — "I think he likes the stuff! That's good, to kinda get that seal of approval. He's one of the most fantastic singers ever. I think what he was taking from was those black singers like Wilson Pickett and Otis Redding. It was just his interpretation, and I think I've got this separate interpretation. There are similarities, and I see it, so it was pretty amazing that he mentioned it." To add insult to ignorance, Josh has even said, "I didn't know who fucking Led Zeppelin was until I was in high school". (Not buying it, dude.)

Josh's twin brother and guitarist in the band, Jake, adds, "I think you got the best compliment. Considering he's an old, grump English guy." Josh also had this to say, "Oh, it's interesting, because there is a lot of those commonalities. Even if it exactly wasn't an overwhelming influence of ours, it still was influential, and we can certainly see it. But overall, it doesn't really affect the writing of our music." So how does he justify that sentiment when he has also said, "I went through a year of really intensely studying what Page did to the point where I knew how he thought." (Wow. That's some balls right there. Some of the best guitarists I know still listen to Page in amazement and say "wow, what was he thinking?") Ok, time to listen to Greta Van Fleet… (be right back…ok, heard enough.)

Separate interpretation? Not an overwhelming influence? (Are you f#ckin' kidding me?)

I realize these kids are young (19–22 years old across the band), but there is simply no way they can make these claims with a straight (or honest) face. Come on, dudes. Own up.

If you don't hear Zeppelin getting knocked off like Nikes in China on songs like "Safari Song" and "When the Curtain Falls", you need to turn in your forty-year-old concert tees.

Plant said they are *Led Zeppelin I*. I hear this plain as day on the single "You're the One." The echoes (and most of the chords and song structure right down to the chorus and the background organ) of "Your Time is Gonna Come" hit me so hard in the face I had to go blow my nose. I watched them play this tune on SNL and grabbed my guitar and played along perfectly, having never even heard it before (much to my daughter's chagrin).

Then there's "Highway Tune", which Josh claims to have written the opening riff to when he was 14 years old (while Dad was blasting Physical Graffiti somewhere else in the house, Josh?). A solid song, no doubt, but again the influence is just too much to get a pass on. In "Age of Man," there is literally a lyric that says, "to wonderlands and of Ice and Snow." (We know who comes from the land of Ice and Snow, and it ain't four kids from Michigan.) Is it just me or is "Flower Power" the discarded take for "Hey, Hey What Can I

Do" that got stuck in the tape machine? (God, they are even biting *Coda* outtakes — which is an album of outtakes!)

I'm dazed, but not confused.

There is a very distinct element to Led Zeppelin which is very hard to escape. Anyone who has ever tried to write a guitar-based song since 1968 understands the impenetrable brick wall that Jimmy Page created and how hard it is to get around without being tagged with "sounds too much like…". Page was just so creative and prolific (even when he was cribbing riffs himself) that he kinda sucked everything into the Zep vacuum. The most successful guitarists coming after Page were the ones who had no choice but to struggle with the comparisons until they found their own voices, and now some of those survivors are actually optimistic about Greta Van Fleet.

A recent voice in support of this young band is Alex Lifeson. At the January 19 Rush Fan Day event at the Rock & Roll Hall of Fame, Lifeson offered this, "At first, I thought — obviously, the influence of Led Zeppelin," he said. "But it's a new time for them, so many decades later, so they're developing their own audience. We were a bar band, really. We had our influences. Certainly, Zeppelin was a big influence for us. But once we got out and we got a chance to play and develop our own stuff and start writing our own material…well, you know, that's history. And I see that with them too. They're young enough that they can carry that banner for a rock band into the future."

Slash weighed in on GVF (I hate that I just did that) during an Australian radio interview. "That whole phenomenon is pretty interesting and cool. It's really opening the doors for a lot of young, new bands — of which there are tons of — that just can't get any kind of traction. So, it's really cool that those guys are making such headway."

Now, in the efforts of fairness (ugh, I hate being fair), Zeppelin wasn't an unequivocally original band when they hit the scene. Their first album (which I had on 8-track so I had to listen to the whole album every time…so retro-cool) borrows heavily from their own predecessors. It's got two Willie Dixon blues tunes, "You Shook Me" and "I Can't Quit You" ("How Many More Times" clearly borrows some old blues tropes, as well); "Babe, I'm Gonna Leave You" was a folk song written by someone else and previously recorded by Joan Baez; "Dazed and Confused" eventually (legally) had to add an "inspired by" credit; and even "Black Mountain Side" was arranged from a traditional Irish folk instrumental (but gets a Page credit). This is the album that Plant feels GVF (ugh) borrows mostly from? It's probably the least Zeppelin-ish album of all from the standpoint of original music but was undeniably the birth of the Zeppelin "sound", which is what's really at play in the GVF conversation.

Led Zeppelin has been entangled in songwriting/copyright disputes quite a few times (ok, at least ten) for everything from the blues-based tunes, like "Whole Lotta Love" (again, Willie Dixon) to "Boogie With Stu" (the Estate of Richie Valens sued for "Ooh, My Head" — which Valens most likely stole from Little Richard's "Ooh, My Soul") to the most contentious — the "Stairway" suit over "Taurus" by Spirit. (Lots of money involved in this one. Just got a new trial ordered in September 2018.) But again, it's not really just the songwriting that we're talking about with GVF. What's really getting on people's nerves (well, at least the people who grew up on Zep) is the collective shrug of these four young dudes who seem to say "yeah, so what?" with every strum and howl.

If you think that Led Zeppelin is solely about loud guitars and heavy drums, you have missed the boat. Yes, the big riffs, the primal vocals, the showy solos, they're all in there, but the real key to Led Zeppelin is what happens in between. While "Heartbreaker" and "Whole Lotta Love" might elbow each other for highlights on Led Zeppelin II, for the fan paying close attention, it's things like "Ramble On" and "Thank You" that add depth and nuance to the band. Each album brought more and more of this, and by *Led Zeppelin IV* we got the full realization of what Zeppelin was destined for.

From "Black Dog" (the quintessential killer riff tune) to "Going to California"(oh, the possibilities of dropped-D tuning), it's all on display. "Stairway to Heaven" puts all of those elements into one tune that builds brilliantly with each verse until it reaches what is arguably the greatest rock guitar solo ever recorded, which segues into one of the more awesome jam out chord progressions ever given to garage bands, and finally culminating in a guitar outro that is so creative and spectacularly arranged that it still offers something different with each listen, followed by a timeless vocal presentation reminding you of how gently the song began. You want it to start over as soon as Plant's voice fades.

Then, two albums later, came the defining moment of Led Zeppelin's evolution—*Physical Graffiti*. It's bold, it's powerful. It's killer guitar work, a blowout Bonzo extravaganza, Plant in top form, and JPJ being used to his fullest (most under-rated member of the band). Two albums full of everything Zeppelin represented musically, lyrically, creatively, and even visually (great album cover and design). Exemplified in the simple perfection of "Kashmir", this album is pure (and let's face it, peak) Led Zeppelin. *Physical Graffiti* ties it all together.

If you're gonna sound like Zeppelin, it's gonna be because of something on this album, more than any other.

So…when a band gets tagged as the "next" Led Zeppelin, man, that's a heavy load and you better be up to the task (and own up). While the influences across some bands coming up were subtle and eventually evolved into sounds of their own (like Lifeson said about early RUSH), some bands were so obvious, they were doomed before they even started. The most blatant perpetrator was Kingdom Come, a German band who must've thought people had somehow forgotten about Led Zeppelin because that tune "Get It On" was so laughably contrived that it got them the nickname "Kingdom Clone". Page wasn't a fan of any of the imitators, particularly the Germans, saying, "Obviously it can get to the point where it gets past being a compliment and it can be rather annoying. When you've got things like Kingdom Come, actually ripping riffs right off, that's a different thing altogether."

Another band that I found to be so blatantly derivative, if not outright shameless, but was so close to home that they got a total pass — Bonham. Fronted by Bonzo's own son, Jason, their song "Wait for You" is just a freaky "dare to compare". After that band ran their short course, Jason knocked around for a bit before eventually filling his father's bass drums for certain special occasions (hat's on to Junior, he did well). Now he just accepts his apropos position as the leader of Jason Bonham's Led Zeppelin Experience.

Then there's Whitesnake.

I openly admit that I really like David Coverdale. He was awesome with Deep Purple, and the early Whitesnake was really great (come on, anything with Ian and Paice and then Cozy Powell is worth it). But that hugely successful 1987 *Whitesnake* album pretty much just threw caution to the wind and said, "We'll be the closest thing to Led Zeppelin you're ever gonna get, so just deal with it." And I did. Guilty as charged. It's a great album, right down to the use of violin bows on the guitars in the stellar, "Still of the Night". Hell, if you loved Zeppelin, and they were gone, this was a pretty damn good substitute. It was so good, it even got Robert Plant pissed.

He would refer to Coverdale as, "David Cover Version" (that's some funny shit). And like all things that burn too bright, Whitesnake devolved into another rock and roll mess of personnel changes and cases of hairspray, and that was all she wrote. (I didn't bother with the next album.)

I don't buy the Heart comparisons to Zeppelin. Heart had to go through Page's brick wall, but they really had their own thing going on right away that was more akin to the times than actually ripping anyone off, and they ALWAYS shouted out Zeppelin as the blueprint. Their live version of "Rock and Roll" was an honest tribute, not a bogart, and it was great. Besides, if anybody could keep up with Plant, it was Ann Wilson.

There were some more recent victims of "Next Zep" name calling, like Wolfmother, an unsuspecting band from Australia who had no idea what was coming for them. I think Lenny Kravitz tried to bogart Zeppelin unapologetically, even recruiting JPJ on some tracks. For some of us New Yorkers and our Big Easy Eskimo brothers, Zebra got a bit of that label mostly because of their incredible live Zeppelin covers, but I don't think it's fair to paint their album work with that brush. I really don't hear it. After a lot of listening and thoughtful reflection (I do that every now and then), I have come to the conclusion that they're more of a greater Wishbone Ash than a lesser Led Zeppelin. I don't buy the comparison on bands like Soundgarden or Foo Fighters. Zeppelin is in the DNA of all that music, but those bands did their own thing, and did it well.

So, back to Greta Van Fleet. Their original Musicpage booking info from 2013 states—"Greta Van Fleet is a blues influenced rock n roll band picking up where classic rock left off."

(Eye roll and groan, but…)

...after some more thoughtful reflection (oops, I did it again), and at the urging of smarter people than me (like Alex Lifeson), I have decided to wait it out before declaring these brash young Motor City madmen blatant apers of the greatest rock band of a previous generation. I will put their youthful ignorance and reckless disrespect aside (for now) and see if they can, in fact, evolve into their own true selves.

"Our environment, the current times, a lot of that influences our music," Jake says. "I think our generations see that and say, 'Oh, this is rock 'n' roll for us.'"

"Rock n' roll for us..." That's a serious mantle to take on. I wonder if young Jake realizes how much is riding on the success of his band, for all of us. Let's face it; the bands of our generation are gone. More of the greats from the '60's and '70's die off each year (seems like each day) and they're not being replaced in-kind. We shouldn't have to rely on "classic rock" stations to provide the soundtrack for our future. We need to be patient, let the young kids play and see what makes it out of the sandbox.

According to Slash, "The thing is, there's a really cool energy right now for new Rock' n 'Roll bands — and it's the right kind of energy, because it's kids that are doing this for the right reasons. It's not about getting on MTV, it's not about fame and stardom, it's not about Learjets and chicks, because none of that shit exists anymore. It's all about the music and it's about the passion of just doing whatever it takes to be able to get your music out in front of people. So, I'm really inspired about what's going to be happening over the next two, three to five years, and coming out new music-wise."

So, I offer this: Maybe Greta Van Fleet should instead follow in the footstompin' musical groundwork of another American Band from their own backyard who made good: Mark, Don and Mel — the original garage band from Michigan.

Grand Funk Railroad found their sound early and gave us plenty of great music without having to endure living up to a "next" anything comparison (their "Heartbreaker" is nothing like Zeppelin's). Do this and maybe people will lay off and let you figure it out...at least for a while.

Rock On.

Originally Published Mar.13, 2019

Pound for Pound

Why drummers are the hardest working musicians in Rock and Roll

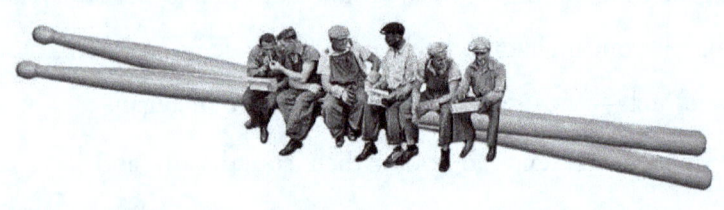

On August 1st, 2015, a momentous event occurred in the world of rock music. It may have passed under the radar of many people, but few drummers will forget it. That date marked the last ever concert by the timeless, inimitable, and arguably greatest power trio ever (sorry HANSON fans) — RUSH. And it's not just that RUSH came to the realization that their popularity had waned. It's quite the opposite. Their albums still went gold, and their concerts were sold out. The truth was the simple and admirable admission by an always classy and humble man that his body just could not handle it anymore. He was physically spent from 50+ years of drumming. The tenure of one of the greatest rock drummers of all time came to end, not because of death, but because of life. That night in Los Angeles was the final drum solo from the great Neil Peart. Long live the Professor.

Unfortunately, Neil Peart is not an isolated case. Drummers having to give up their passion is not uncommon, and the more prominent and successful ones are not exempt from the physical stress that comes from a musical talent that punishes the body as much as the instrument, no matter how many back-up musicians or drum machines are employed. Phil Collins, possibly the most successful rock drummer in history as the only one in the rarefied air of artists having sold over 100 million records both as a solo artist and member of a group (McCartney and Michael Jackson are the other two), was forced to retire in 2011 due to health problems related to drumming. After back surgery to repair a damaged vertebrae, the resulting nerve damage prevented him from even holding drumsticks (and if you don't think the back problem came from drumming, just ask a drummer). He's finally returned to performing, but he walks on stage with a cane, and sits during the show. He doesn't drum.

Singers and guitar players (bass included) are always out there, center stage, running around, posing, posturing, laughing and sweating (oh so photogenically). Some of that sweat is earned from the aforementioned activity, but realistically, it's from the stage lights (those suckers get hot). The stage-stealers' physical activity is entirely up to them. Granted, we come for a show and expect all this hoopla, but there in the back, behind a wall of wood, chrome and Mylar is the hardest working member of that show. The freakin' drummer (earned sweat aplenty). Two arms, two legs going full force for two hours or more, no muscle group left out. The drummer is laying the groundwork for everything else going on, the veritable heartbeat of the band. If the singer flubs a lyric or the guitar player hits a bad note, eh, nobody really notices, but if the drummer loses that back beat, oh shit! look out, everyone in the house stumbles. Then when the rest of the band needs a break, just throw in a drum solo so the guitar player can grab a beer or the singer can take a leak (drummers apparently never have to piss, they just sweat it out, which is why drummers are the only other group of people besides basketball players for whom sweatbands are made).

While Todd Rundgren might play it down (of course, he's a guitar player), banging on the drum all day is definitely work. According to Livestrong.com, "a study from Chichester University, and quoted in a 2008 article by the BBC, noted drummers can elevate their heart rate up to 190 beats per minute, which is comparable to the top heart rate that many elite athletes experience while playing their sport. The study revealed that drummers must have top-level endurance to perform." They go on to estimate that one hour of drumming burns around 250 calories (hmmm...I'll dub that the "Charlie Watts" workout). Studies at Harvard and Oxford say that drumming can lower blood pressure and improve cognitive brain development (uh...I know some drummers...not sure about the brain part of the study). There is even a trend (ahem, fad) of Cardio-Drumming classes that claim recorded calorie burns of 600–900 calories per hour (now we're talking the "Dave Grohl/ Nirvana" workout. Comes with a neck brace and a tube of Ben-Gay).

Even pretending to drum is a workout. While air guitar (unfortunately a real thing) requires no more than hanging your arms by your side, slouching at the shoulders and fake strumming against your leg while bopping your head up and down (insert sarcastic eye-roll), air drumming demands much more — you actually have to lift your arms and move them (and yet it stills seems as nerd-ish as air guitar, let's face it). Air drumming at RUSH concerts is to be expected, if not mandatory, during "Tom Sawyer." (Interestingly, Peart has said that "Tom Sawyer" is the hardest song to play live and not because of those drum rolls. It's because the drum pattern never repeats. Every measure and bar are unique.

Check it out. It's unbelievable, and nearly impossible to follow…at least for mere mortals.)

If you need a Hollywood backdrop to reinforce the brutality of being a drummer, have a look at the movie, *Whiplash*. (Talk about blood, sweat and tears.)

Ok, we get it. So, it's no accident that the Muppets' drummer is named Animal, but how did we go from a former Liverpool hairdresser getting the greatest gig in the world to Tommy Lee spinning upside-down in a cage?

Early on in the rise of rock and roll bands, the setup was pretty much the same: singer, two guitar players, a bass player and behind them, on a relatively standard four-piece kit sitting on the floor, was the drummer — a nondescript guy who got recruited probably because he actually owned a kit. The only thing that even drew your eye in the direction of the drums was the band's logo painted on the front skin of the bass drum. Drummers as band leaders was unheard of outside of the jazz world, where some of the greats, like Chick Webb, Buddy Rich, Gene Krupa, and Art Blakey, just could not be ignored, but with the British Invasion came that head flopping dude just happily banging away while the singers and guitar players were front and center. Some early drummers were even placed off to one side, literally clearing center stage for the others.

Two guys unapologetically changed all that, bringing a physicality, intensity and notoriety to rock drumming that no one saw coming.

The first one of these game changers literally blew up the image of the laid-back drummer. Obviously, I'm talking about Keith Moon. While The Who got tagged as stage hooligans early on, with Townshend's guitar-smashing, amp-destroying live antics, Moonie took it that one step too far (as he always did) and put a bit too much explosive in one of his two bass drums (another sonic and visual innovation) and made television history in 1967 on the Smothers Brothers' show by causing a blast that momentarily knocked the show off the air and reportedly started Townshend on the road to partial deafness. That kind of stuff got Moon noticed, but arguably for the wrong reasons. As crazy as he acted (and played), he was actually changing things musically. "My Generation" is generally remembered as a milestone for bass players, with Entwistle's bass "leads" causing a revolution of their own, but Moon is also rewriting the role of the drummer on that tune. He is essentially leading that track to all of its landmark elements from the bass breaks to Daltrey's stuttered vocals. Continuing with "I Can See for Miles," and escalating in every way from "Bargain" through "The Real Me," Moon ushered in an era of controlled chaos that undeniably stepped up the game for lazy drummers and seat warmers worldwide. Tragically, we will never know how long he could have gone on like that. Just like some "elite" athletes, Moon also employed the use of PEDs (wink and a nod) in those epic rock performances. He abused his body physically in so many ways that even as The Who prepares for yet another tour in 2019, you just have to look at how hard 53-year-old Zak Starkey works to fill those shoes and wonder if a 73-year-old Keith Moon could have kept up with Moonie from 1967.

The second drummer in this dynamic duo is Ginger Baker, the man who effectively created the drum solo as an art form. Baker refused to be limited by whatever impression the establishment had for what a rock drummer should be. His kits were expansive and unique to his style with his mounted toms perpendicular to the floor, not angled toward the inside. You saw Baker in the center of those drums, not behind them. Interestingly, he was with Moon at a Duke Ellington concert in 1966 where they saw Duke's drummer using double bass drums. Moon then went out and bought a second Premier kit while Baker had to wait for Ludwig to make one for him. Right out of the gate with Cream, Baker let the music world know that drummers were not accessories or mindless timekeepers and he punctuated that with "Toad" — his five-minute drum solo track on Cream's debut album.

Neil Peart has said of Baker: "His playing was revolutionary — extrovert, primal and inventive. Every rock drummer since has been influenced in some way by Ginger — even if they don't know it" ("primal" hits it right on the head). Ginger Baker pushed himself hard and it wore on some of his band mates. The rumor was that Clapton started jamming with Steve Winwood after the demise of Cream and was glad to get some distance from the mercurial Baker, but Ginger heard about the sessions and showed up, resulting in the short-lived band, Blind Faith, from which Clapton promptly exited. Baker continued on after Cream with other projects, but ultimately did reunite with Bruce and Clapton in 2005 and seemed to do a fine job with his old material, but it finally caught up with him, and now at age 79, with heart problems and osteoarthritis, Baker's played his last gig. The title of a documentary about Ginger kinda says it all — *Beware of Mr. Baker*.

So, with the door kicked wide open, in came the next heavy hitter — John Bonham. Instead of the double bass drum set-up, he up-sized the bass drum to 26", went with two floor toms and never looked back. When standard drum techniques were not cutting it, Bonham spared no pain to get where the music needed to go. On "Moby Dick," he sets aside his sticks and goes hands on (you could hear the beating his hands were taking with every slap. Those were not congas, they were Ludwigs with metal rings). After Page nearly gave up on "Four Sticks," Bonzo saved the song by holding two drumsticks in each hand to create the drum track, hence the title. That Bonham bass drum is as much a signature as Plant's voice. The intro to "When the Levee Breaks" is possibly the best opening to any Zeppelin song. (Turn it up, step back and be awed.) Bonham's sheer thunder was the driving force behind much of the Zeppelin catalog, but his nuance was just as brilliant. If you think the drumming on "Kashmir" is anything but masterful, try listening to it from a new perspective by pushing the melody back and letting the drums move to the foreground. You'll hear a drum track playing in 4/4 over a 3/4 guitar and string track. It's why that simple riff holds such a grip (it's all about the bass...drum). Bonham was more about following Page than JPJ. That synchronicity is what made so many of those songs, like "Black Dog" often imitated but never duplicated. Bonham was tragically, another monumental talent that we would never get to experience as a Lion in Winter.

James Brown earned the nickname, "The Hardest Working Man in Show Business," and allegedly would lose two or three pounds each time he performed as he toured incessantly, especially during his height in the late 60's. Brown was a tremendous stage presence: singing and dancing with the energy of ten men, but he had to have a beat to dance to. While James was upfront, whether or not there was a melody, there was always a groove, and that groove was supplied by the original "funky drummer," Clyde Stubblefield. Clyde held it down right there with James every night. So have a look behind that "hardest working man" and you just might notice another hard-working guy keeping up.

Behind every decent band is a good drummer, behind every good band is a great drummer and behind the great bands are the legends: Moon, Baker, Bonham, Palmer, Peart, Ward, Paice, Bruford, Cobham, Copeland, Beauford, Grohl, Ulrich, Smith; and then there are the ones who spread the wealth to multiple bands, like Cozy Powell, Mike Portnoy, Zak Starkey, Simon Phillips, Gavin Harrison, Kenny Aronoff (to name but a few); and ultimately those few in a class by themselves as studio guys like Steve Gadd, Peter Erskine and Vinnie Colaiuta.

So, as much as we want our musical idols to stay young forever and tour endlessly, we need to accept that these people (especially the drummers) are not machines, and sooner or later, they need a break. They have bodies that break down like ours, they get sick like us, and yes, they die. More importantly, they have lives beyond letting us cling to our youth for another night, they have families that might want them around now, after thirty or more years on the road kept them away. We will always want more, but sometimes, expecting it is just unfair. The music they gave us will live forever, so we should appreciate that and let them live out their lives, let them age with dignity, let them rest in peace.

Rock (and Drum) on.

DEAD ARE ALL THE GODS (PARTS 1 AND 2)

Originally Published Apr 13, 2019

Send More Musicians, Keep the Geese, Eh?

Why music, not weird bacon, might be Canada's greatest export

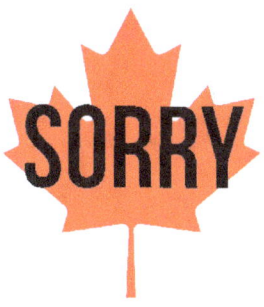

In the early 60's, the American music scene was subject to the loud, brash and all engrossing British Invasion. According to the Encyclopaedia Britannica (that's British/Latin for — "we know everything"): "These charming invaders had borrowed (often literally) American rock music and returned it — restyled and refreshed — to a generation largely ignorant of its historical and racial origins." (So, they were "charming", and we were "ignorant"? How about I return a restyled and refreshed middle finger back at ya, Britannica.com.) Crowds of young Americans gathered en masse at airports, fainted at concerts and reportedly flung some underwear at the "charming" scamps as they dominated the charts and minds of America. So, while most of the "ignorant" Americans were preoccupied, there was another smaller, quieter, yet very significant invasion of sorts happening.

While some of our citizens were taking off to the Great White North to seek a more conscientious solution to the Vietnam War (ahem…dodge the draft), some young folks were actually heading south with an equally honorable approach of their own — changing the world through music. No fanfare, no fainting, just great tunes. I present to you — the *Canadian Infusion:* the non-invasive exchange of incredible musical talent flowing down from our peaceful neighbor to the north that occurred nearly simultaneously with the British distraction of the 1960's and continues to this very day across genres and platforms with Canadians breaking traditional, streaming, downloading and digital single records, and snatching Grammy, CMA, AMA, Billboard and MTV awards (those are still around?) by the armloads.

The list of Canadian conspirators is longer than you might think, and though the real pioneer could be argued to be Ottawa's own Paul Anka (who charted at #1 with "Diana" in 1957), I feel that if we're going to compare it to the onslaught of British artists, it should start with Neil Young.

Neil Young came to Los Angeles in 1966 and immediately began a musical journey that has hit upon nearly every genre and produced some of the longest lasting songs in each one.

For what it's worth, his output with Buffalo Springfield gave us the near-classic, "Mr. Soul"; his Crazy Horse days resulted in *Everybody Knows This is Nowhere* (pick a song, any song on this album); then, with CSNY, came *Deja Vu,* an album in a class by itself, with the standout Young song, "Helpless," pretty much cementing his reputation as a song-crafter extraordinaire. He even wrote what might be the most prominent protest song of the Vietnam Era — "Ohio". Since then, in every iteration, Neil Young has been incredibly prolific and influential (though if I hear one more weekend guitarist/lawyer with a $3000 Martin and a pair of Merrells singing "Old Man" in a bar I'm gonna hurl). The interesting thing about Neil Young is his unique signature as both an acoustic artist and an electric one. The fact that he took "Hey Hey My My" and turned it into two distinct songs exemplifies his genius. The "Out of the Blue" version displayed his folksy soul, while "Into the Black" earned him the distinction, "Godfather of Grunge" (even down to the flannel shirts). No one will argue against him having a very, uh…unique…quality to his electric guitar work (his nickname "Shakey" supposedly came from his early camera work…hmmm), but as "Rockin' in the Free World" is frequently covered live by Pearl Jam, Satriani, and Vai, you can't deny it's a great guitar tune. Neil Young just defied labels and did his own thing (even if it pissed off some Southern Men who heard Mr. Young singing and were inspired to write a "Sweet" song about him. Nod, nod, wink, wink, eh?)

As a kind of neat fit with Neil's folksy side came his fellow Canadian, Joni Mitchell. After little commercial success and limited opportunity in Toronto, Joni headed for America, weaving her way from Detroit (a lot of Canadian bands first broke on Motor City radio stations in the 70's and Cobo Hall is right up there with the Fillmore and the Garden) through the East Coast and finally to Florida, where David Crosby saw her and took her back to Los Angeles. Her undeniable talent as a songwriter, singer and guitar player (she uses a lot of non-standard tuning, confounding standard tuners everywhere) finally resulted in *Clouds*, which won a Grammy in 1969. Her masterpiece, Blue, dropped in 1971 and to this day is considered one of the top 30 albums of all time and the #1 album by a female artist ever.

From their 1968 debut, *Music from Big Pink*, to their 1976 farewell, *The Last Waltz*, leave it to a bunch of Canadians (all except Levon Helm, an Arkansas boy) to write some of the most quintessential American songs in music history. After morphing from the Hawks to Dylan's backing group to their own thing, The Band earned that stand-alone moniker with Robbie Robertson, Levon, Rick Danko, Garth Hudson and Richard Emmanuel living up to the name. Clapton allegedly wanted to join up after Blind Faith disbanded but ended up worming his way into Delaney and Bonnie instead (pale imitation, Eric). Pretty much anybody who loves a great song will sing along to "The Weight" and...aaand...aaaand...take that load off Fanny.

A bit of a hybrid, Steppenwolf gets Canuck cred because of its members. Founder John Kay, an Ontario native, but non-Canadian citizen, brought the pieces of his Canadian band, The Sparrows, down to California, revamped in 1967 and turned "Born to be Wild" and "Magic Carpet Ride" into garage band staples in perpetuity.

As the sound of music left the matching suits and haircuts of the British Invasion behind, a band of Canuck brothers, who with the addition of a bass player (recommended by fellow Canadian Neil Young), were the blue-collar answer music fans were ready for, and in 1973, Randy Bachman and Fred Turner launched Canadian guitar rock into overdrive. After pretty decent success with another Canadian band, The Guess Who, guitarist Randy Bachman took a song that his previous band had rejected and turned "Takin' Care of Business" into a rock classic that by 2011 had become the most licensed song in the Sony Music's publishing catalog. (For perspective, this catalog includes the Beatles, Stones and Michael Jackson). Bachman Turner Overdrive went on to sell over 30 million albums worldwide (and even more copy paper and pencils for Office Depot).

1974 brought together three dudes under four letters that changed progressive rock and keeners lives forever — RUSH. (All hail Lerxst, Pratt, and Dirk. 'Nuff said, eh?)

Then along came another great Canadian power trio, Triumph, whose Allied Forces, Never Surrender and Thunder Seven albums all went gold ("Fight the Good Fight" is just a flat-out great song). Montreal's Frank Marino and Mahogany Rush was literally a juggernaut (loudest concert I ever attended — L'Amour's in Brooklyn) that showed the "headliners" at California Jam II (oddly held in a town named Ontario…) how to put on a live rock performance. Marino is a guitar player favorite and perennially underrated virtuoso, just listen to 1988's Double Live to understand why. April Wine first cracked the American charts with their second album, *On Record*, in 1972, and continued with Canadian chart toppers in the 70's while garnering some American attention with songs like "I Like to Rock," then produced the internationally multi-platinum *The Nature of the Beast* with "Sign of the Gypsy Queen" in 1981. Four multi-platinum albums in the 1980's get Calgary's Loverboy into the mix. "Working for the Weekend" makes quite a few guilty pleasure sing-along lists (come on, you know enough Labatt's will get you using a beer bottle as a pretend mic).

Ontario's Bryan Adams had a big run in the 80's with a constant stream of radio friendly rock hits, but Reckless really put him over the top in 1984. "Run to You" had a very cool guitar riff pulling in the rockers, and "The Summer of '69" seemed to play on an endless loop in car stereos, but when a tune from his next album ended up in Kevin Costner's *Robin Hood* movie, Adams exploded. "(Everything I Do) I Do It for You" was a worldwide #1 and since then, Bryan Adams has gotten every award, national medal and hall of fame nod created and has sold over 100 million records. That's a lot of loonies (Canadian dollars, not fans).

As for guitarists in the late 80's, I don't think anyone will disagree that Jeff Healey was beyond special. Just listening to *See the Light* was like a gift from Guitar Heaven, but when people started witnessing (because that's what it was) his talent, you could not believe what you had just seen (which was also amazing because he couldn't see it either, being blind from the age of one). With Jeff's guitar on his lap and his fingers stretching from his thumb to his pinky across the fretboard, the sheer range of his playing was impossible to replicate. A true original and a tragic loss for all. (Grab a copy of the movie *Roadhouse*, fast-forward past Patrick Swayze, and just watch Jeff's performances in the bar. That's no movie magic, just Jeff doing his thing.)

The 90's continued to bring some interesting new musical ideas to the table, like Barenaked Ladies, and their truly inspired #1 hit, "One Week," which had people singing about Chinese chickens and laughing at funerals, and k.d.lang's Grammy and MTV award winner, "Constant Craving," but let's face it, there was one Canadian that owned that era — Alanis Morisette. *Jagged Little Pill* was her third album (her first outside of Canada), and when it dropped in 1995, it was a killer. "You Oughta Know" cleared the table and it seemed that every other tune on the album just went right to the top. She was everywhere, and deservedly so. *Jagged Little Pill*, the first Canadian album to ever achieve double diamond status, sold 33 million albums (and counting), won five Grammy Awards, including Album of the Year, got her an engagement ring from fellow Canuck Ryan Reynolds (pre-Dead Pool), and ultimately landed her the role of God in Kevin Smith's *Dogma*.

Alanis ruled the Rock roost, but another Canadian woman was making waves elsewhere and she got a brief nod for "rocking by association." Shania Twain was breaking into country music when she was heard by one of the great rock producers — Robert "Mutt" Lange. Mutt was the genius behind AC/DC's *Highway to Hell* and the legendary *Back in*

53

Black albums, for which he gets eternal cred. While Mutt shouldn't get the credit for Shania's natural talent, he did co-write and produce her next two albums, which were historic successes. The second of these, *Come on Over*, became the best-selling album ever by a female in any genre.

Canadian women kept crushing it as Sarah McLachlan closed out the 90's with *Surfacing*, picking up two Grammy awards, launching the Lilith Fair concert tours featuring only female solo artists and female-led bands and raising 10+million for charity. Her hit "Angel" went on to become the soundtrack for the most heart-wrenching series of ASPCA commercials ever (my own dog hides from the guilt of her cushy life when that song starts). Nelly Furtado's *Whoa, Nelly!* sold 9 million albums in 2000 on the back of tunes like "Turn Off the Light" and "I'm Like a Bird," and then in another genre-bending left turn, 16-year-old Avril Lavigne became the face of the "Pop Punk" movement with her skate punk persona and massive hit "Complicated," which went to #1 in several countries. Now, at 34, she's the third best selling female Canadian artist with 40 million albums and 50 million singles sold and the youngest female soloist to have a #1 album in the UK. (Now, I'm not saying that fellow Canadian pop punk rockers Sum 41 bogarted the Avril steeze, but guitarist Deryck Whibley was married to her for 3 years during their peak. ABD, dude).

All of Indie favorite Arcade Fire's studio albums were Grammy nominated and the principal members got an Oscar nod for scoring the film, *Her*. Feist kept the women-who-rock category alive with a Best New Artist Grammy nod in 2007. Three Days Grace post-grunged themselves into multi-platinum albums in the U.S. and Canada.

Now, while this article is mostly centered on rock and rock-adjacent musicians, a brief aside should also acknowledge International mega-star Celine Dion (that one song probably earned enough money to raise the freakin' Titanic), crooner Michael Buble (just for the silly name), jazz pianist Diana Krall (wife of Elvis Costello), troubadour Gordon Lightfoot (launching a new world tour for his 80th birthday — yes, 80!), reluctant folk legend Leonard Cohen (for giving every contestant in a vocal competition a chance to mangle "Hallelujah"), soft-popper Anne Murray (for helping me spot all the Canadian "Snowbirds" in Boca), and rapper Drake (for culling the herd of morons who tried the "KiKi" video challenge on Facebook).

There's a sense of, "oh, really?" followed quickly by, "whatever," when it comes to finding out that someone you've enjoyed listening to for years is Canadian. Canadians are truly the closest thing Americans have to cousins, so family is family (trying selling that to a French-Canadian — Déguelasse!). And as we dread the annual reappearance of the only true Northern invaders — the Canada Goose and Justin Bieber — we will weave through the minefields of fecal droppings and endure the constant squawking of them both, all the while singing Montréalais Corey Hart's "Sunglasses at Night" and being grateful that the geniuses behind NAFTA (or the USMCA or whatever it's called now) never considered a tariff war over music.

Rock on, eh?

Originally Published May 8, 2019

Pull My Finger(s)

The Eddie Van Halen/Thelonius Monk Correlation

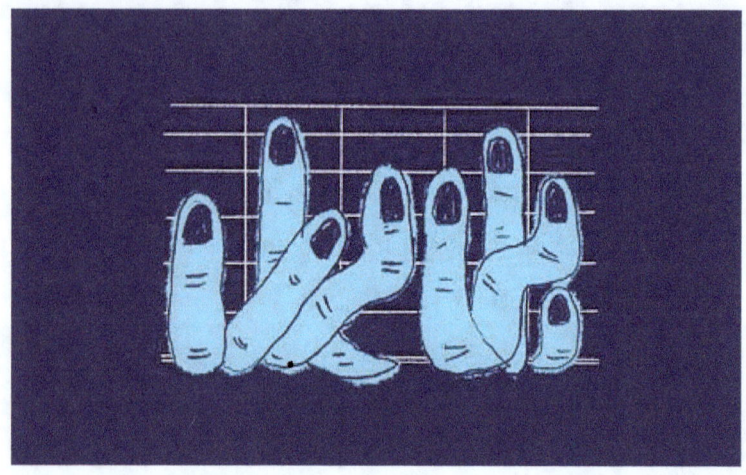

Accompanying the current *Play It Loud* exhibit of original guitars and gear used throughout the history of modern rock at the Metropolitan Museum of Art in New York City are video testimonials by some of the artists on display: Jimmy Page, Keith Richards, and Eddie Van Halen, in particular. Each of these artists use their own words to explain their approach to playing, writing, finding the perfect tone, and generally creating music. The artists interviewed each represent very significant milestones across different eras and to say they have merely influenced rock music would simply be ignorant. Page, Richards and Van Halen quite literally created modern guitar rock (which is why they are

57

prominently featured). This section of the exhibit also includes each artist's actual playing and recording rigs: guitars, pedals and all. (To say this equipment is priceless is another gross understatement.)

So, there they are, chatting on giant screens about guitars and such, and each one had a very surprising thing to say about their styles and the lack of traditional or conventional methods behind them. Keith Richards, known for using alternate tuning on his five string "Macawber" Telecaster (primarily open-G: GDGBD) and strumming away happily, acknowledges that this is not something someone formally taught him, it's something he discovered from other players he encountered along the way and then employed himself to create some of the most enduring riffs in history. He very amusingly (in his equally unique half-man/half-cigarette pirate speak) tries to give some really deep explanation as to why he prefers the tuning before he laughs and admits that the simple fingerings are just easier and "I'm lazy". (If you look at his currently arthritic, gnarly knuckles, those fingerings probably also extended his career by twenty years.)

As Jimmy Page talks about his guitars and his setups, you can see his hands mindlessly noodling with bits from "Ramble On" and "Whole Lotta Love" and if you watch instead of listen, you'll see him finger the chords to these songs in ways that would have guitar teachers apoplectic. (He flat-fingers his E-chord in the 7th position with his pinky. Makes no sense: limits your other fingers, uncomfortable for the wrist, yet created some of the longest lasting riffs in history, so who's the real dummy here?),

Then Eddie Van Halen puts it most plainly—"Ninety percent of the things that I do on guitar, if I had taken lessons and learned to play by the book, I would not play at all the way I do…" (Wait…so, if Eddie had taken lessons from the old guitar instructor down the block, he might have turned out to be a UPS worker playing in a Cream tribute band on the weekends instead of the most influential guitarist of his generation?)

"You have your way. I have my way. As for the right way, the correct way, and the only way, it does not exist." — Friedrich Nietzsche

Eddie is the truly interesting phenomenon in the pantheon of self-taught players doing strange things with their techniques. While Page and Richards both contributed to the overall change in what was being done with their respective instruments, Van Halen changed how it was being done. There is no question that Van Halen's re-figured (and re-fingered) approach to guitar playing revolutionized rock guitar more than any player that came before (arguably even

Hendrix and Jeff Beck) because it wasn't just a shift in expression or a re-packaging of roots music, it was a complete retooling of methodology. There was no subtlety. It was loud and brash, inventive and adventurous. It wasn't a matter of what you were playing (blues, jazz, pop), it encompassed any style you wanted to use it in, but it was not easy. Where Keith chuckles about being "lazy," Van Halen's approach was anything but. You could either do it, or you couldn't. No low-hanging, easy-to-strum, cool-looking guitar. Van Halen's guitar is up high where the work gets done. He needed to get both hands all over that fretboard.

Eddie said about his early guitar days, "I used to sit on the edge of my bed with a six-pack of Schlitz Malt talls. My brother would go out at 7pm to party and get laid, and when he'd come back at 3am, I would still be sitting in the same place, playing guitar. I did that for years — I still do that."

While he openly concedes that he did not invent the two-handed tapping style, he certainly retrieved it from the obscure and unnoticed space where it was floundering and introduced it to the rock and roll masses through a very loud amplifier and with the most unorthodox example of instrument-building ever seen. Oddly enough, he explains in his MET video segment that he was inadvertently inspired by seeing Page doing a one-handed trill during a concert at the

LA Forum. He then realized that if he moved his right hand above his left as he did this same trill, he could effectively clamp down on the neck and move the nut down the fretboard at will as he played the same simple pattern…and it sounded cool. Building on this, he began using either hand as a makeshift capo while tapping further down on the same string, creating an exponential number of notes and a very distinct sound. While recording the first album, producer Ted Templeman heard Eddie doing a workout of this style while warming up with Alex and asked, "What was that?" After Eddie explained that it was just a little bit he used to loosen up, Ted said, "do it again" and recorded it. That 1:42 warm-up — "Eruption" - changed guitar playing forever.

Ok, so rock guitarists can't keep their fingers where they belong. Big surprise there.

Not so fast…before Eddie found the guitar, there was another finger fiddler who did it his own way, on a piano.

Playing piano since age six and mostly self-taught, Thelonius Monk had a more than forty-year career, received a Grammy Lifetime Achievement Award and a special Pulitzer Prize for his innovation and impact on the evolution of jazz. He won the DownBeat Critics Poll in 1958 and '59. He is one of only five jazz musicians to be on the cover of Time magazine. And he is one of the most controversial talents to ever break it down, and that controversy was…his fingering style.

Monk invited the wrath of centuries of piano teachers with knuckle-rapping-rulers at the ready, just waiting to unleash the punishment of inches upon any student who dared to splay or "flat-finger" the keys. Arching the fingers (holding the imaginary tennis ball) is the first thing you learn (and are punished for ignoring) before you are even allowed to touch a key, and of course there are reasons for this traditional approach: less tiring, less cramping, better accuracy; but nevertheless, Monk flat-fingered his way into history. Bob Doerschuk wrote of Monk in Keyboard in 2017, "To someone like Monk, these same old keys might seem to fit only the same old locks. To get inside new doors, a new combination had to be found." Thelonius Monk found the combination. His unorthodox fingering would allow him to hit one key with two fingers, hit two keys with one finger, he would unleash seemingly unintentional seconds, he improvised with parallel sixths. Critic Paul Bacon wrote in DownBeat, Monk "has the most expressive feeling I can find in any musician playing now, but it has cost Monk something to play as he does … 50-percent of his technique. He relies so much on absolute musical reflex that Horowitz's style might be unequal to the job."

Monk's style was innovative, unique, certainly not traditional or conventional and definitely not appreciated by all. Audiences who were used to more familiar sounds in their music had a lot of trouble with Monk's style. Even his legendary collaborator, Miles Davis, asked why he persisted with the "weird chord changes" that just "sounded wrong." Some said he played as if he "was wearing work gloves." When not flat-fingering, Monk would hold his hand high above the keys (another alleged no-no) and come down hard into a chord with a percussive attack that prompted others, like poet and jazz critic Philip Larkin, to dismiss him as "the elephant on the keyboard." His unusual fingering style invited noticeable dissonance as scales and modes clashed for the attention of his touch. Juilliard-trained composer Hall Overton countered the critics of Monk's unorthodox approach, explaining that he "adjusted his finger pressure on the keys the way baseball pitchers do to the ball to make its path bend, curve or dip in flight."

So where did all this funky fingering get Thelonius Monk? He is the second-most-recorded jazz composer after Duke Ellington, which on its face may not seem remarkable, but when you consider that Duke has over a thousand compositions to choose from and Monk has roughly seventy, well, no further explanation needed. See ya, "Round

Midnight". (He also owns one of the best quotes ever... "The piano ain't got no wrong notes." Perfect.)

Much like Monk did on the piano, Eddie Van Halen also employed dissonance (melodic, not sonic, which he also exploits to great effect) to accompany his technique, but Eddie's is one case where it may have been more irrational exuberance than intentional musical disruption. Since his arrival on the scene and unbridled deconstruction of traditional guitar thought moving forward, the "Eddie Van Halen" scale has emerged. (Eat that, Mel Bay)

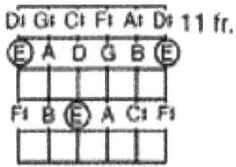

This is more of a playing convenience than an actual musical consideration, utilizing a symmetrical three-note pattern over minor and major keys, no matter your position on the neck. It's like his fingers were just moving along so fast, he couldn't bother to form a more sensible scale out of fear they might get tangled into a knot he could never undo, so...look out. The inclusion of conflicting degrees (b3 and 3, b7 and 7) would be obvious (and undesirable) in a slow-picked solo, but when played at a high speed and palm-muted (oh, yeah...and VERY loud) the result is, uh, really cool! This type of soloing also tends to work best over a simple bass line, often no more than a root note just thumping along in the background with no rhythm guitar track risking potential exposure of the very real deviation from the actual key they were playing in. With just a plodding E back there, you can switch between major, minor, or whatever other scale floats your boat and nobody would be the wiser.

A lot of really good traditional guitarists got left in the dust once the newer generation of players embraced the Van Halen technique, but when that dust finally settled and the early imitators had run their course of overkill, the tapping technique found its place with the true artists who know when and where to use it. Melody and structure dictate when to bend, when to tap, and when to just play it straight. Clones who couldn't escape the accompanying hair band scene that rose simultaneously eventually dispersed into obscurity. Some players, like Night Ranger's Jeff Watson, actually expanded the tapping palette, developing an eight-finger technique with both hands on the fretboard at the same time. It was interesting and unique, but it pretty much lived and died with Jeff's participation in the band's initial success. Some players like Nuno Bettancourt and Warren DiMartini (who weren't necessarily clones, but more victims of the times) still garner respect and minor audiences. Paul Gilbert, Andy Timmons and Greg Howe managed to cull individual identities from Eddie's wake and are still tremendously creative artists and incredible players to this day. Joe Satriani and Steve Vai can wield this technique like no others, but it's not the only tool in their box, which is why they are so revered as players and future legends themselves. (Unlike Eddie, Steve was actually trained…by Joe Satriani!) Michael Hedges (gone too soon) paved the way for odd fingerings on acoustic guitars and his spirit is still felt in players like Andy McKee and Kaki King.

Ralph Waldo Emerson said "Do not follow where the path may lead. Go, instead, where there is no path and leave a trail."

When a musician goes where there is no path, they don't leave trails, they blaze a super-highway, so let's hope that the next time a music teacher sees or hears a student doing something out of the norm, they skip the ruler, give it a beat, and see where that kid is going with their "weird" chords changes and funky fingers. We have enough UPS workers; we need more Eddie Van Halens and Thelonius Monks.

Rock on.

Originally Published July 10, 2019

White Rabbits, Nixon, and Chick-fil-A

How Grace Slick unabashedly ushered in the age of the female rock star

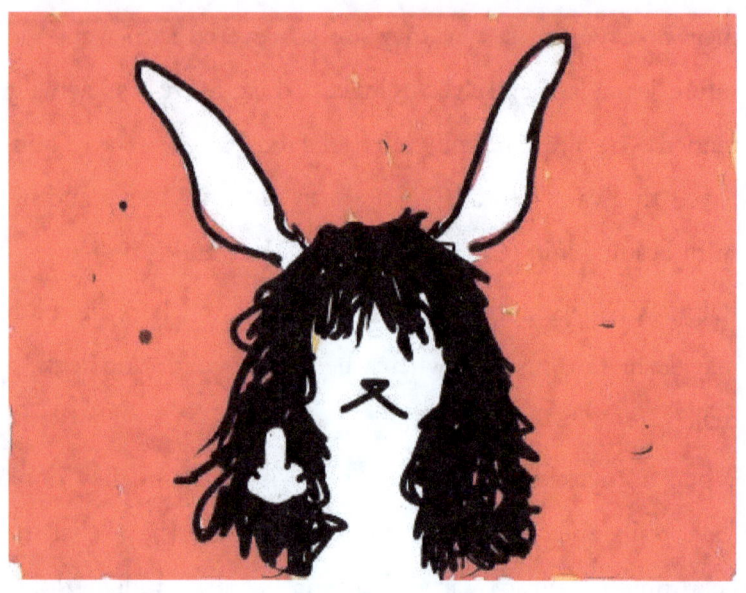

"I'm getting ready to sing. Some guy in the audience shouts: 'Hey Gracie! Take off your chastity belt!' I look directly at him and say: 'Hey, I don't even wear underpants.' I pull my skirt up for a beaver shot, and the audience explodes with laughter. I can hear the guys in the band behind me muttering: 'Oh, Jesus.'" — Grace Slick recalling a Jefferson Airplane show in Chicago in 1973

Rock and Roll is about power — metaphorically and literally, and one thing is for certain, the more powerful the messenger, the more power the message conveys. In nearly every case, that messenger is primarily the singer — that person front and center delivering the surge of energy you came to receive. It's that energy, that power and that freedom that makes all the difference. Their vibe becomes your vibe. Sitting politely during a musical performance and sipping wine during intermission is for opera at the Met; jumping up and screaming in a weed-scented Madison Square Garden is for Rock and Roll. When a singer pulls a note from somewhere down deep and pushes it out with the force of all the air in their lungs, phew…that's it right there. The power of Rock and Roll. Amen.

While male rock stars, especially lead singers, were considered the founders of the emerging rock scene of the late 60's, there were several women - two in particular - who were delivering the type of killer vocal performances that the men wouldn't catch up to until Robert Plant stepped up the men's game on *Led Zeppelin I*. Some of those early male rock singers brought many things to their music, but pure booming vocal power was not in their toolbox. They employed sex appeal where their vocals were simply interesting, like Jagger (a "mouthy" kind of vocalist); or were buoyed by masterful songwriting, like McCartney (who used more of a roll-the-words-around-in-the-cheek approach than a deep wail) or Lennon (who kinda bounced his voice off his teeth). Eric Burdon might be the earliest one to really have that "from-the-gut" style. When people think about powerful female singers from the late 60's and 70's, Janis Joplin is pretty much the first one that comes to mind, and she would definitely be a correct choice, but she would not, and should not, be the only choice.

The other correct choice is Grace Slick.

Janis Joplin's performance of "Ball and Chain" at the Monterey Pop Festival in June of 1967 is widely considered her breakout moment. Lou Adler, one of music and film's most influential producers of the time said "…as a vocalist, her performance at Monterey was also one of the great concert performances of all time." Interestingly, there was little mention of the performance by her band, Big Brother and the Holding Company. It was all Janis. Yet, before that career making moment, another debut turned heads in the male-dominated rock scene and a new message was delivered. That message was "the women have arrived!" and that messenger was Grace Slick.

Grace Slick made her live debut with Jefferson Airplane at the Fillmore auditorium in San Francisco on October 16, 1966, nearly a year before Janis exploded at Monterey Pop. It was arguably the turning point for Jefferson Airplane and was even released as a special live album, *Grace's Debut*, over forty years later. Her first studio recording with Jefferson Airplane, *Surrealistic Pillow*, was released in February 1967, and represented a new direction for the formerly folk-inspired group toward the emergent "psychedelic" rock scene of San Francisco. The two singles on which she sang lead were hits right out of the gate. "Somebody to Love" and "White Rabbit" propelled the group onto the national scene on the back of not only Slick's songwriting, but her undeniably powerful vocal performances (just check out the isolated vocal tracks on YouTube).

Grace Slick was a bit of an anomaly on the Rock scene up to that point. Women making waves in the Rock and Roll ground zero of San Francisco were not pushing the limit like Slick. Folk music had Joan Baez and Judy Collins. Joni Mitchell was pushing boundaries, but flat-out Rock-star-quality wailing and larger-than-life personalities were still in the waiting...until Grace. West Coast archivist Alec Palao wrote: "More than anyone else, she was the most original and unique talent to emerge from the whole San Francisco 1960s milieu." Grace was the poster girl for the Monterey and Woodstock era but never saw herself as an icon.

"Women have always been singers. Female Supreme Court judges, that's impressive. I just thought I was a singer — not Bach or Mozart or Handel. 'Course, if we were all singers we'd be in terrible shape. Where would the farmers be? The Airplane let me sing. God bless America for that."

The big difference between Grace and Janis was the supporting cast. Janis was Janis Joplin and they were Big Brother and the Holding Company, regardless of how they were billed (again, consider the Monterey Pop reviews). While Janis stood apart from her band, Grace Slick stood out amongst her bandmates. She contributed songs and shared lead vocal opportunities with Marty Balin both in the studio and on the stage. Throughout her career with fellow band-mate Marty Balin, it seemed that whenever the song called for a softer touch, like the song "Miracles," Marty sang, but when it needed that extra something, it was all on Grace. (Talk about role reversal. Case in point: "Fast Buck Freddie" and "Ai Garimasu" from the same album, *Red Octopus*.)

"Marty was never very communicative, which is odd when you're singing duets. Maybe he was jealous of me 'cos I was so fabulous. He's the only one [of the band] I never speak to anymore."

Not to be outdone by her contemporary male rockers, Slick also partied hard and raised eyebrows like a rock star. Being outrageous wasn't only a playground for the boys. For a performance on *The Smothers Brothers Comedy Hour*, Grace wore black face and raised the Black Panther salute. She wore a Girl Scout uniform (which she also wore on the cover of Life magazine) and a nun's habit on stage. In 1969, she was to attend a function at the White House where she intended to slip LSD into President Nixon's tea. If her accomplice, Abbie Hoffman, hadn't been denied entry, she might have pulled it off. Slick also had her share of troubles with the law while part of Jefferson Airplane, getting arrested at least four times for what she has referred to as "TUI" ("talking under the influence") and "drunk mouth. And she was never shy about literally exposing herself to the fans (the Chicago "beaver" incident mentioned above was one of many).

"Jim Morrison…he got arrested for being obscene. I didn't. So, when women do it, I guess they think it's less offensive to see tits, than to see a dick. I don't care either way. Dicks are good, tits are good."

While the '70's began to claim the lives of her contemporaries (Janis died in October of 1970, and Jim Morrison the following July), 1974 saw Jefferson Airplane become Jefferson Starship after the departure of founding members Jorma Kaukonen and Jack Cassady, who went on to form Hot Tuna. Jefferson Starship, now primarily spearheaded by

Grace and Paul Kantner, found continuing success with the latest incarnation of the band (eight gold and multi-platinum albums including *Dragonfly*, *Red Octopus* and *Spitfire*, and Grace's solo career produced a Grammy-nominated album, *Dreams*), yet the band began to crash land due to infighting over touring (Marty Balin) and the excesses of alcoholism (Grace), and by the end of 1978, Jefferson Starship found itself without either of its singers. During the Europe tour in 1978, the first night of the German concerts was canceled due to Grace's condition and on the second night, Grace was wasted yet again and mocked Germany from the stage for losing WWII, causing a fan riot. She left the group the next day. In 1979, the band released its first album without Slick or Balin, *Freedom at Point Zero*, which amazingly went gold on the strength of the single, "Jane," sung by former Elvin Bishop vocalist Mickey Thomas.

Grace on her eventual sobriety: "It wasn't easy. Being sober is weird. *People* magazine broke my anonymity about AA, but it wasn't a surprise. My behavior made that obvious. Everybody knew I was a big drunk. Plus, booze and cocaine is an ugly combination. I loved it. I lived on it, because the two things even each other out. Then you do more. I could afford it. Coke was so cheap, and we were Rock'n'rollers. Who cares? I only stopped when you couldn't get the uncut stuff from German pharmaceutical chemists. I was a snob."

Grace Slick returned to Jefferson Starship by 1981 and by 1985, after the departure of the last original Jefferson Airplane member, Paul Kantner (and a nasty lawsuit), Grace Slick owned the rights to the band name. The remaining band continued as Starship, which had tremendous commercial success, peaking with "We Built This City," which in 1985, made Grace Slick, at 46 years old, the oldest female singer with a Billboard #1. She bumped Tina Turner (44 yrs. old with 1984's, "What's Love Got to Do with It?") and beat herself the following year at 47 years old with "Nothing's Gonna Stop Us Now." She held that distinction until 1999, when Cher took the mantle at 53 years old with the #1 song, "Believe." As successful as Starship was, Grace left the band in 1989.

"That was a sell-out band. The Airplane was a smorgasbord, but the Starship I hated. Our big hit single, "We Built This City," was awful. What are you talking about? What city? LA was built on oranges, film and oil. San Francisco was built on the gold rush. The Romans built London. It sounded like we were bragging, even though Bernie Taupin, an Englishman, wrote the lyric. I could sing it — and the others — because I can fake enthusiasm. You have to act to get on stage. I felt like I'd throw up on the front row, but I smiled and did it anyway. The show must go on."

During her retirement, Grace Slick did occasionally appear onstage with Paul Kantner for a Jefferson Airplane reunion, and she still found her way into some classic rock star incidents — like getting arrested in 1994 for pointing an unloaded gun at a police officer — but her singing career was finished on her own terms.

"I don't like seeing people my age leaping around, singing about their feelings when they were 23," she says. "If you're comfortable with it, go ahead. I'm easily embarrassed for people. 'Oh my God, honey, get off the stage. Become a producer or something...I feel that rock and roll is not an old person's medium. They look silly. Yeah. You're not hitting the notes you used to be able to hit. Because everything is falling apart when you get old. Your voice is not as good. You don't look right. Generally, you haven't picked out the right outfit, because you have on...like an Eighties jacket."

Grace Slick was inducted into the Rock and Roll Hall of Fame in 1996 as part of Jefferson Airplane and wrote her memoir, *Somebody to Love? A Rock-and-Roll Memoir* in 1998. She has spent her recent years as a painter and artist, but most recently caused waves in 2017 when Chick-fil-A, a corporation with a well-documented stance against gay marriage, approached Grace for the right to use "Nothing's Gonna Stop Us Now" in an ad campaign. She initially refused, but then accepted and donated all the proceeds to Lambda Legal, the largest national legal organization working to advance the civil rights of LGBTQ people, and everyone living with HIV.

She told Forbes in February 2017: "See, I come from a time when artists didn't just sell their soul to the highest bidder, when musicians took a stand, when the message of songs was "feed your head," not "feed your wallet." We need that kind of artistic integrity today, more than ever."

Grace Barnett Wing Slick made her debut in October of 1966 and ended up in the Rock and Roll Hall of Fame. It was a long, strange trip from San Francisco to Cleveland, and hard-earned every step of the way, but it was a destination that was all but assured that night at the Fillmore thirty years before. While we all know the power and impact that Janis Joplin represented, she left the stage in 1970 and in many ways, left it up to Grace Slick to remind every young female singer just what it took for a woman to endure and succeed in the man's world of rock and roll. Grace Slick was not a diva or a Queen, she was a hard-working, hard-living rocker and that made her something better than either of those things —

it made her an equal to every one of her contemporaries, male or female. Grace Slick was a rock star in every sense of the word, and will always be; and we will always remember what the dormouse said...

Feed your head!

Originally Published Sep 6, 2019

Sympathy for the Devils

Were the Rolling Stones actually the best band of the British Invasion?

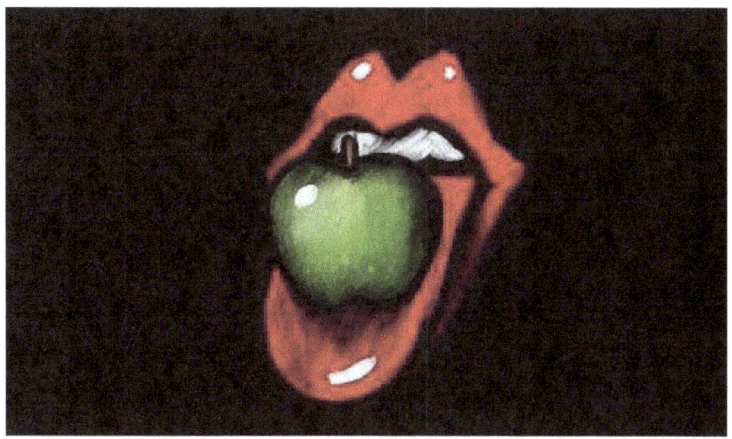

There has been a decades old dialogue about which band was better: the Beatles or the Rolling Stones? Such discourse should seem ludicrous when you're talking about something as creatively subjective as music, but once the Beatles showed up to insane crowds greeting them at airports, history-making appearances on Ed Sullivan, and a Shea Stadium concert that no one ever actually heard due to the screaming crowd, the whole "invasion" became more of a phenomenon. And, like any phenomenon, it warranted a curious eye for cultural, social and economic impact. As is to be expected, when the Beatles became a marketing miracle and a money generating machine, promoters were desperately looking for the next Beatles-level act to cash in on.

Enter the Rolling Stones...

When the Fab Four were asking to hold your hand, the Stones were pitching spending the night together. When John was asking for Help!, Mick suggested painting the whole world black, and while Paul was lamenting that he couldn't buy love, Mick complained how he couldn't get no satisfaction. While the Beatles sang of love and hope, the Stones went for the jugular, singing about sex; nervous breakdowns; mothers (not just their kids) doing drugs - real life stories. The Rolling Stones were all about sex, drugs and rock and roll right out of the gate, and they told you so in their music.

Meeting The Beatles…

But was there really any rivalry between the two groups? Were the two groups of youngsters from post-WWII Britain really such opposites? It doesn't appear to be so. Much of this talk was promotional strategy coming from record labels and managers back in the earliest days of the British Invasion. It was Brian Epstein and Andrew Loog Oldham who directed the rise of these two bands. Epstein signed the Beatles during their Cavern Club days and it was his idea to craft the clean-cut style of neat haircuts and matching suits that made them famous, but the 19-yr old Loog Oldham, who had previously worked at Epstein's NEMS organization, invoked the "Anti-Beatles" image after initially dressing the Rolling Stones up in matching attire for their television debut before realizing the value in making them stand out as non-conformists.

But again, that was managers and promoters, not the boys in the band themselves. It was, in fact, George Harrison who encouraged Decca Records executives to check out the fledgling band after Decca had famously skipped signing the Beatles in the first place. Decca signed the Rolling Stones soon after, and John even gave one of his early tunes, "I Wanna Be Your Man," to the Stones to record instead of the Beatles. Throughout their peak years in the 60's, the members of the two groups supported each other frequently: Mick and Keith during the "All You Need is Love" video, John at the "Rock and Roll Circus" broadcast, for example. Of course, there were little pissy moments about "copying the Beatles" and such, and they did enjoy some friendly musical and artistic competition at times, but that mostly ended when they each became distinct and original voices of their own, not just Brits imitating American rock and roll and covering Chuck Berry and Little Richard. (Thankfully the Stones knocked it off after the silly *Satanic Majesty's Request* album cover essentially mocked *Sgt. Pepper's*, right down to images of the four Beatles hidden in the cover art. Their own album art took off incredibly after this with the original art for *Beggars Banquet* getting rejected for a more record-label acceptable cover, and ultimately, *Sticky Fingers*, possibly representing the pinnacle of album cover design to date.) And even the architects of the supposed rivalry — the managers and record executives — worked out the timing of album and single releases and live performances so as not to step on each other's success. (After all, let us not forget, "Money don't get everything, it's true…What it don't get, I can't use.")

There is no wiggle room in the fact that the Beatles catalog is the greatest collection of songs ever written (213 original songs). Time has proven this to be true over and over again. It is such a deep well of incredible songs that even reissues, remasters, anthologies, compilations, previously unreleased live albums, soundtracks, and even covered versions are all guaranteed to be certified gold and beyond. (Talk about a ringer, the 2000 album of all Beatles number one songs, *1*, became the worldwide best-selling album of the decade at 31 million sold and counting, and this was an album celebrating the 30th anniversary of the band's break-up! Who says breaking up is hard to do?) Ultimately, the Beatles have sold 600 million albums to the Stones 240 million, and recorded twenty #1 songs to the Stones eight, but does this really answer the question of which group of musicians were the better band? The Rolling Stones have been an active recording and touring band from their formation in 1962 up until the present day, just finishing what might be their last concert on August 30, 2019, fifty-three years nearly to the day of the Beatles final concert on August 29, 1966.

Were the Beatles ever really a band, though?

The Beatles of the Cavern Club days were certainly a band. They were covering the rocking numbers of the day for just enough cash to get by. They were hungry and they were eager to play for as long as people let them.

Even in their early Beatle-mania days, after being re-packaged by Epstein, replacing Best with Ringo, and taking America by storm, they seemed inseparable as a band. They were The Beatles.

Then came "Yesterday."

"Yesterday" foreshadowed everything that was to come for the Beatles from that point forward. It announced to the world that the Beatles were as much individuals as they were a group, maybe even more so. It has been made obvious over the years to everyone who has ever heard a Beatles song that "Yesterday" was not a Lennon/McCartney composition. "Yesterday" was Paul McCartney's song. Paul wrote and performed what was to become the most recorded song in the history of popular music—by himself. There were no other members of the band on the track, but there was a very significant second person involved—producer George Martin. There would be little disagreement in stating that George Martin was as integral to the innovation and creative progression of the Beatles as any individual member of the band. Yes, they wrote the songs, but George Martin was the visionary genius who knew how to steer them from great songs to musical masterpieces. None of the members of the band had the technical expertise or experience to incorporate the elements of string arrangements (next up after "Yesterday"—the sheer genius of "Eleanor Rigby") and studio innovations like adjusting tape speeds for effects (that's not a harpsichord solo on "In My Life," it's a sped-up piano), reverse tape and splicing ("Strawberry Fields Forever"), bouncing multiple tape tracks (pick anything on *Sgt Pepper's*). Forget Brian Epstein, George Martin was indeed "the fifth Beatle." It was after "Yesterday" that people began to recognize the nuances in Beatle songs that identified who wrote them. It was more than just who sang the lead, it was in the lyrics, in the chords, in the attitude, and occasionally, in the anger. George Martin knew how to bring out each personality in the studio. Even in the midst of the strong presence of John Lennon and Paul McCartney, George

Harrison was able to exert his own identity and songwriting prowess. Given the same weight as his bandmates, George may have just been able to prove himself their equal, but his input was curtailed by John and Paul. (George Harrison wrote roughly 10 percent of the songs in the Beatles catalog, but his songs hold 20 percent of just about every top ten list of that catalog. "Something" became the second most recorded Beatles song after "Yesterday," though Elton John declared the song "better than "Yesterday," much better." "While My Guitar Gently Weeps" speaks for itself.)

So, it became apparent that the collaborative part of the band gave way fairly early on to the individualistic part and only became more so as the years wore on. Considering this, is it tenable that the Beatles truly stopped being a "band" soon after Beatlemania and turned into the most successful songwriting collective in musical history?

Jagger/Richards bore no such resemblance to the Lennon/McCartney dichotomy. This was a true collaborative effort. The lyrics and the tunes were perfectly matched. Could "Paint It Black" or "Honky Tonk Woman" be any more perfectly in sync? And where the Beatles were a primarily a melody-driven band, the Stones were a riff-driven band (though the Beatles did pull off a good riff every now and then — cases in point, "Day Tripper," "Hey Bulldog," and

"Helter Skelter"). Keith Richards was unquestionably the "riff master," and Jagger's lyrics were the perfect match. "Jumpin' Jack Flash" without either the lyrics or the riff is just nowhere near the same song at all. The Stones were also a blues-rock band, while the Beatles were more in the pop-rock vein, and this resulted in a sexier, more visceral approach to songwriting. The bad boy image gave them a certain license through the years. John Lennon caught holy Hell for mentioning Jesus Christ, yet Jagger sang as the devil, and wrote about war, murder, drugs and slavery. (Even Mick says there's no way he would write anything like "Brown Sugar" today.) "Gimme Shelter" is a timeless, gritty rock song that the Beatles could never have pulled off. Could you even picture Paul writing the "rape, murder" lyric sung by Merry Clayton — the greatest back-up vocal performance in the history of rock and roll, which essentially made Jagger the guest vocalist on the track. In the 70's, Jagger even invoked "some Puerto Rican girls, that's just dyin' to meet you." Never raised an eyebrow.

The Rolling Stones continued on successfully as artists for years after The Beatles broke up. This could even be argued as the Rolling Stones peak era. Every Stones Album post-Beatles has gone gold and/or platinum, they charted eight #1, and two #1 singles. *Sticky Fingers* and *Exile on Main*

Street are as close to perfect albums as it gets. Yet, the ex-Beatles also continued on as "solo" artists (nod, nod, wink, wink) to great success as well. Paul had 25 albums solo and with Wings (fake Beatles). He produced ten #1 US/UK albums, fifteen #1 US/UK singles, something around 70–100 million albums - nearly every one gold or platinum. John, in the short 10 years before his assassination, had 7 gold or platinum studio albums (two #1 and four #1 singles) and gave the world, "Imagine," his greatest song and best possible example of why he is still revered to this day. George came out of the Beatles with the most headwind of them all. He recorded the triple-album extravaganza, *All Things Must Pass,* dropping a #1 single, "My Sweet Lord" and a top ten, "What is Life?" It was a #1 album that offered songs that were rejected by The Beatles, proving that George had as much to give as the others, but was limited by the group itself. Even Ringo killed it. He had two #1 singles and 3 gold albums, and still tours with the always popular All Starr Band. So, can we view this ongoing output from the Liverpool gang as a loose-knit band? Maybe, but loose knit doesn't count when the Rolling Stones are still around. Keith Richards famously, and ironically, said, "no one should leave this band except in a pine box." True for Brian Jones, but not so much for Mick Taylor, who lasted from 1969–1974, before being replaced with Ronnie Wood; and original bassist Bill Wyman, who left in 1993.

So, the better band?

Well, it seems as if the Beatles were destined to break-up from the minute they hit the U.S. shores. Beatlemania had fans taking sides right from the start and the media loved it. We're still trying to pry apart the band with polls picking the "favorite" Beatle and analyzing what that says about you as a person. The record label didn't help with things like the promotional posters in the White album — not a group shot, but four separate photos of the individual members. Even the "Paul is dead" myth and the *Abbey Road* cover showed the distance between them. Paul wasn't dead, The Beatles were.

Or were they...

Is it possible that despite the official "break-up" which ended their joint recording career, The Beatles, through continuing to record as solo artists and occasionally bouncing off each other's orbits, never truly broke up musically? Have all their years as solo artists really just amounted to what would have been Beatles albums after all? Think on this for a moment. Paul, John and George all wrote songs for and played on the *Ringo* album (his peak studio work). Ringo was in Paul's *Broad Street* movie (possibly Paul's nadir). "Maybe I'm Amazed" is clearly a residual Beatle tune, and just imagine (no pun intended) "Mind Games" as a Beatle track. There's a great perspective on this in the movie, *Boyhood*, in which Ethan Hawke's character presents to his son, an unofficial "compilation" of songs by Beatle members since their break-up. Dubbed, *The Black Album*, it's presented as a specific and well thought out track listing that gives some serious credence to this concept. It suggests, if not proves, that The Beatles lived on long past 1970.

The Rolling Stones have been a rogue's gallery of rock and roll excess since the beginning, but they accomplished the most important part of being a band — staying together. 57 years and counting. Sure, they're down a few men, but the core is alive and well (Ron Wood counts, he's been in there for 45 years now).

Does any of this answer the question we started out on? I don't know, but like the man said, "You can't always get what you want, but if you try sometime, well, you might find, you get what you need."

So, if you need an answer, here it goes:

The Rolling Stones were the best band to come out of the British Invasion, in part because they simply outlasted the Beatles.

…or did they? (*The Black Album* reveals all.)

Roll on.

Originally Published Nov 25, 2019

A Star is Bored

When actors act like musicians…and the world shrugs

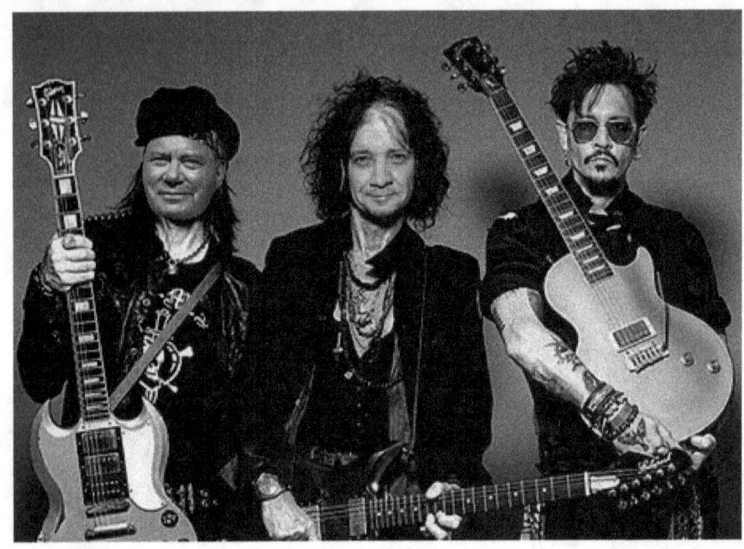

In 2019, an album of original tracks, *Rise*, was released by a band that started out in 2015 covering Classic Rock songs, such as "School's Out" and "Whole Lotta Love." The band is led by three highly successful artists: Aerosmith guitarist Joe Perry, long-time rock veteran Alice Cooper, and…Johnny Depp

(Wait…is this a musical group?)

(Yes, hang on, let me finish.)

They call themselves, Hollywood Vampires, and Johnny Depp is their guitarist and occasional vocalist.

(Captain Jack Sparrow is the leader of the band?)

(No, that's a character he plays. He's an actor. But he did supposedly model that character on Keith Richards, so...maybe. Let me continue.)

Johnny even has a signature guitar with specially wound pickups of his preference made by the Duesenberg Guitar Company.

(What's this now, he even designs guitar pickups?)

(Well, kinda. They designed them and he said, "Oh, that sounds cool." Okay...)

So, Johnny Depp, three-time Academy Award nominee, ten-time Golden Globe nominee and winner drops an album of original music.

(Based on his pedigree, the album must be a killer!)

(Well...not so fast.)

Even with the help of Joe Perry, who represents half of one of the most successful singer/guitarist duos in rock history (with Steven Tyler), and the vocals and stage presence of the inimitable Alice Cooper himself, Depp's vanity project peaked at 184 on the US Billboard 200 chart. There have been some live performances and a short tour in 2016 (where Joe Perry collapsed on stage. All those years of drugs and excess with Tyler — the so-called "Toxic Twins"-- and hanging with Depp almost takes him out...pure rock and roll irony), but rock history was not made. Now, maybe that wasn't the goal, but if it was just about hanging out with pals, then why the hype? Jam in your mansion's 10-car garage.

(Ok, so one actor chases a dream of being a rock star. Actors are people too. It's not like they all do it.)

(If only that were the case.)

In 2019, two-time Academy Award, Golden Globe and Screen Actors Guild nominee Jeremy Renner decided that the best way to accompany a wildly successful acting career (dude's part of the Marvel machine) was with…an album of original songs. Yes, Hawkeye went from the highest-grossing movie in history, *Avengers: Endgame*, to not-the-highest-grossing album in history, *Main Attraction*. (The title track did end up in a very confusing JEEP commercial though.) This year also saw the release of the 7th studio album, *Speck*, from The Boxmasters, the band featuring an actor with more than 70 major wins or nominations for his work in film: Billy Bob Thornton. For his contributions to music…uh, none that I could find.

Now, this does not say anything about these actors' love for music or their right to pursue whatever creative outlet they want to pursue, but it raises an interesting question: why do great actors make such mediocre musicians, while great musicians seem to have incredible critical and financial success when they decide to act?

Case in point #1: (albeit an obvious one, though more will be discussed).

In 2018, a highly anticipated film starring an award-winning musician was released, garnering major acting award nominations and wins for the performer. The film was *A Star is Born* and the actress was Lady Gaga. The nine-time Grammy winner was nominated for Best Actress by the Academy Awards and Golden Globes. By all accounts, after some smaller roles and TV appearances, she had made an incredibly successful transition from the top of the world of music to the top of the world of film. Can you discount some of this because she was actually playing a musician in the film? I don't think so because her character in the film was a pretty clean departure from her Gaga persona (with the possible exception of the drag bar scenes), but there are many instances dating further back than this that are even better examples of the musician-to-actor transition.

Case in point #2: Frank Sinatra

After some small cameos, Sinatra was cast opposite Gene Kelly in *Anchors Aweigh*, a film that garnered several Academy Award wins. He appeared twice more with Gene Kelly, to great acclaim again, but these films were all musicals, and not much of a departure for Sinatra or an indication of his ability as an actor. That all changed with his Academy Award winning role in *From Here to Eternity*. Sinatra won Best Supporting Actor for his performance (which not so coincidentally revived a slumping singing career). The *Los Angeles Examiner* noted that Sinatra is "simply superb, comical, pitiful, childishly brave, pathetically defiant." They called his death scene in the film "one of the best ever photographed." Now, he did return to musicals to keep his singing career in the spotlight, but he also played a psychopathic killer in the film, Suddenly; and was nominated for an Academy Award for Best Actor for his portrayal of a heroin addict in *The Man with the Golden Arm* in 1955. Not necessarily musical heartthrob roles, but definitely great acting choices.

<u>Case in point #3:</u> Cher

No conversation about Lady Gaga's crossover success goes anywhere without the groundwork laid down by Cher. A musical novice turned icon, Cher went from a successful singing career with Sonny Bono to television star with *The Sonny & Cher Comedy Hour* (where she won a Golden Globe) to a stellar solo singing career. Then came acting. She earned critical acclaim on Broadway with *Come Back to the Five and Dime, Jimmy Dean,* Jimmy Dean; then an Academy Award nomination and Golden Globe win acting beside Meryl Streep in *Silkwood*; a turn opposite Jack Nicholson in *The Witches of Eastwick*; and ultimately, an Academy Award for Best Actress in *Moonstruck*. (Just for perspective, at the time Cher's singing career was burgeoning in the 1960's, actor William Shatner released his first album, *The Transformed Man* in 1968.)

(If anyone ever said "I loved his version of "Mr. Tambourine Man.", that alone should be game, set, and match for this argument.)

Now, as for dreams deferred (or egos run wild), here's a pretty short list of major movie stars and the bands they front (if you've never heard of them, well…that's pretty much the point):

Kevin Costner & Modern West; Dennis Quaid and the Sharks; Russell Crowe and 30 Odd Foot of Grunts; Jeff Daniels and the Ben Daniels Band; Jada Pinkett Smith and Wicked Wisdom (a female fronted nu-metal band!); the Kiefer Sutherland Band (he gets props for getting the Gibson Guitar Company to make a gold top ES-335), to name but a select few. (There are plenty more.)

There are some notable exceptions (exception being a generous term): Jared Leto had a pretty good run with 30 Seconds to Mars; Jeff Bridges seems to fit his country music leanings (doesn't hurt that he won an Academy Award for his portrayal of a country singer in *Crazy Heart*); Kevin Bacon has been respectably gigging with his brother for years as the duo, The Bacon Brothers; Zooey Deschanel snagged a Grammy nod for She & Him's tune, "So Long"; Jack Black is hard to take serious with Tenacious D, but he's got a mighty passion for great rock music, so he gets a parody-as-respect pass; and finally Steve Martin and the Steep Canyon Rangers. Martin has been a serious banjo player from before his stand-up days, so he gets credit for continuity and actual musical ability.

On the not so notable exceptions side, with multiple worst actor awards, let us not forget that action star and black-belt martial artist Steven Seagal is also a blues musician whose last album, , gave us the timeless single, "Alligator Ass."

However unfortunate and unfair, when an artist who is well known for unique and interesting performances in their noted craft ventures into a new arena, the expectations that follow are high, and when they fail to meet that bar, it is hard to not view their attempt as a vanity project, a novelty act, or just simply, an act. Actors act. It's what we expect, and our unconscious bias will view it through that lens. Should Johnny Depp or Jeremy Renner be lambasted for trying something new? Maybe, maybe not, because we will never know what their expectations or assumptions were, but when they don't meet ours, well…the adoring public turns on you pretty quickly.

Were there some duds as far as musicians in movies? You betcha. (Ever seen an Elvis movie?) Yet, the successes seem to far outshine the dubious efforts of the Hollywood machine to turn matinee idols into cash cows. So, from Captain Kirk to Captain Jack Sparrow, caveat emptor, even when it's your favorite actor's latest music album.

Rock on… *(or act on, whichever applies).*

Originally Published Mar 15, 2020

'Tar liom'

When Rory Gallagher made Irish Guitarists Matter

In 1971, voters in the UK paper Melody Maker chose Irish blues guitarist Rory Gallagher as the International Guitar Player of the Year, ahead of such notable contemporaries as Eric Clapton, Jimmy Page and Steve Howe. At the peak of British guitarists' dominance over rock and their interpretation of American blues starting a resurgence of interest in blues guitar playing, an Irishman with no major record label backing or radio hits captured the attention of not only music fans, but his contemporaries and future guitar greats as well. Queen guitarist Brian May credits Gallagher with giving him his distinct sound, recalling a backstage meeting with Rory in 1970 after attending multiple shows by Gallagher's band, Taste. "I said (to Gallagher), 'How do you get the sound? What is it?' And he said, 'Oh, it's very simple. I have this guitar and I have this amp (amplifier) — an AC-30 amp — and I have this little Rangemaster Treble Booster...'

So, I went straight out and got the AC-30 and the Treble Booster and it gave me what I wanted; it made the guitar speak. So it was Rory that gave me my sound, and that's the sound I still have." Alex Lifeson spoke of opening for Gallagher on Rush's first tour, "I would watch his set and go back to the dressing room and just play, just because I was so inspired by watching him play. Honest to God, his soul was just amazing, and to see him close his eyes and just get lost in his playing was truly, truly remarkable."

William Rory Gallagher was born in Ballyshannon, County Donegal on March 2, 1948, and soon after moved to Cork. His early interest in stringed instruments began on the ukulele, which prepared him for the first guitar his parents would give him at age nine. After winning a talent contest at age 12 and using the money to buy his first electric guitar. He performed with these throughout his adolescence until he was able to put some money down on another electric guitar at age fifteen — a 1961 Fender Stratocaster (yes, that legendary beat-to-hell, unmistakable Strat — Serial Number 64351), reportedly the first one in Ireland. It was ordered by an Irish musician who rejected it because he had ordered a cherry red and a sunburst was shipped instead. The guitar was then sold as second-hand and Gallagher bought it in 1963 for around 100 pounds, a sum Gallagher's mother worried would be a lifelong debt. It wouldn't take long for that concern to subside, and with 30 million albums sold over his career, it proved to be a worthwhile investment. (Fender would eventually offer Custom Shop recreations for $5000.)

The music scene in Ireland in the '50s and early '60s was dominated by Irish show bands - traveling bands of 7 or 8 members, fronted by a lead singer instead of a bandleader, that continuously toured the Irish countryside. It's estimated that at one point there were as many as 700 such show bands touring at the same time. In 1963, teenager Rory Gallagher joined one such band, Fontana. Gallagher slowly influenced the band's direction from pop music to R&B and changed their line-up and their name to The Impact. After The Impact disbanded, Gallagher formed the band Taste, a power trio performing R&B and blues rock, gaining local notoriety for their regular gigs at the Marquee Club in London, resulting in their supporting Cream at their farewell concert at Albert Hall and Blind Faith's North American tour. Taste ultimately broke up just after their 1907 Isle of Wight festival performance, but not before raising people's awareness of Gallagher's arrival on the scene.

While Taste introduced Gallagher to a broader audience, it was the breakup of Taste that opened the door for Rory Gallagher's stellar 20 plus year career of solo work that still astounds to this day. In the 1970s alone, Rory Gallagher produced ten albums, two of them live recordings — *Live in Europe* and *Irish Tour '74*. It was Gallagher's marathon live performances and his dedication to touring that endeared him to his loyal fans and countrymen. Rory Gallagher was a reserved man in private life, but his onstage energy was marveled at by his audiences and peers alike. Rory's brother and manager, Dónal, noted in an article on Gallagher in *The Sunday Times*, "I remember Eric Clapton remarking to me in 1969, during an American tour, on how reserved Rory was. It was strange to have someone that exuberant on stage and so deeply private and introverted offstage." While other artists were warned not to tour Ireland in the '70s due to the extreme political unrest in the North, Gallagher insisted on touring his home country at least once every year.

In 1975, the Rolling Stones were seeking a replacement for Mick Taylor and though Rory went by for a jam, he wasn't interested in the slot, preferring his solo career. In 1972, Gallagher recorded with one of his idols, Muddy Waters, on *The London Muddy Waters Sessions*, which brought Waters a Grammy Award. He also returned to London in 1973 to record with Jerry Lee Lewis on *The Session…Recorded in London with Great Artists*, which became Lewis' highest charting album in nearly 10 years.

Rory proved to be as diverse in his playing as he was dedicated to blues. He could produce straight up rockers, like "Shadow Play" and "Bad Penny" (a hugely underrated classic), then slide effortlessly into a soulful ballad, such as "I Fall Apart," or "A Million Miles Away." His fifth solo studio album, *Tattoo*, was an example of the influences of blues, jazz, folk and country, and the collection of acoustic selections from 1974 through 1994, *Wheels Within Wheels*, demonstrated that an unplugged Rory Gallagher was a completely separate force to be reckoned with. But through all his music, his roots in the blues were undeniable. "I suppose the ultimate dream, aside from wanting to be a good player or having a good band, is that in 50 years' time, one of your songs matched a blues classic," he once said. His take on classics such as, "Messin' with the Kid," and "Bullfrog Blues" became live staples. Clapton once told the BBC that Gallagher should be credited with "getting me back into the blues."

As it too often happens with artists of rare talent, Rory Gallagher died an untimely death in 1995 from complications of a liver transplant at age 47. Gallagher's legacy continues to this day and the legions of artists who credit him as an influence continues to grow.

Joe Bonamassa got a rare chance to play Gallagher's Strat at his London show in 2011. "To sell out London's

Hammersmith Apollo is amazing," said Bonamassa. "Selling it out for two nights? Even better. But to get to play Rory Gallagher's 1961 Stratocaster on my opening date? That's something I would have paid money for. Talk about a once-in-a-lifetime experience."

"The song 'Avalon' on the new record is very much influenced by him," said Slash, who revealed he had met Gallagher in Los Angeles in the mid-80s.

At the time of Rory Gallagher's emergence on the music scene, Irish artists breaking outside of the Emerald Isle were few and far between. Van Morrison, another product of the Irish show band circuit, had found wide success with the group, Them, and their hit, "Gloria," but truly gained worldwide attention with his solo work, "Brown Eyed Girl," and secured that recognition with the album, *Moondance*, and its eponymous single. More on the rocking side of things, Phil Lynott and Thin Lizzy gained momentum with "Whiskey in the Jar," in 1974, but really broke out in 1976 with *Jailbreak*, and the monster hit, "The Boys are Back in Town." Thin Lizzy also introduced Belfast guitarist extraordinaire Gary Moore to a wider audience. Moore proved to be an inspiration for many other guitarists, yet also met an untimely death from a heart attack in 2011 at age 58. The talent was certainly evident in these revered Irish musicians, but Gallagher holds a special place in the pantheon.

Hot Press journalist Dermot Stokes in Marcus Connaughton's biography, *Rory Gallagher: His Life And Times*, said of Rory Gallagher's impact on music in Ireland, "I think that the hugely important thing that Rory did early on in his career was to establish that an Irish band could form, play original material — could do it in Ireland first of all, then could take it to London, then Europe and around the world." The Edge of U2 recalls, "I wasn't even playing guitar, but everyone loved Rory, he signified something for kids of my era — the Irish guitar player, up there with the greats."

Gallagher is honored across his beloved homeland with statues, plaques, music libraries, and street-names across the island, from Cork to Belfast to Ballyshannon, but most fitting is the blues festival held in his honor every year in Donegal. The Rory Gallagher International Tribute Festival 2020 hosts established artists and newcomers every May in Ballyshannon and attracts over 10,000 attendees.

Alex Lifeson summed up Rory Gallagher as well as anyone. "That was the kind of guy he was, it wasn't just about the music in the band and his guitar and all of that stuff. It was his personality and his soul, he was so thoughtful and considerate to other people, so polite. Honestly, he was such a wonderful person, never mind his talents and skills. He was just a really great man. We could use a lot more like that."

Agreed…

Originally Published Apr 26, 2020

Neon Roots, Soul Brothers, and Rainy Days

Is Billie Eilish writing history or righting it?

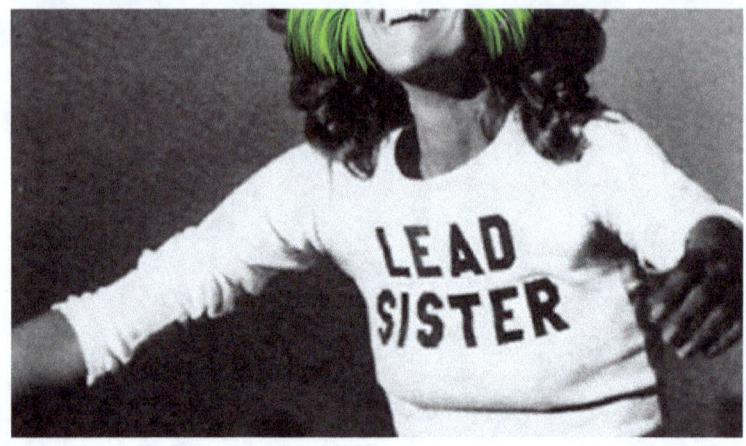

At the 2020 GRAMMY awards in January, artist Billie Eilish won Song of the Year, Record of the Year, Album of the Year and Best New Artist. Her brother, Finneas, also collected five GRAMMYs that night as well; some shared with his sister, some on his own. The last time anyone ran the board of major awards like that was in 1981. This just added to the teen's crowded shelf of American Music Awards, Apple Global Artist of the Year, MTV Video awards, pretty much every award available (including a Guinness World Record, for something…).

Seeming to appear out of the ether (actually SoundCloud), Billie Eilish Pirate Baird O'Connell is another example of digital Beatlemania — near instant fame on a global scale, and the personal toll that comes with it.

Many of Eilish's longtime friends couldn't relate to her newfound fame and, as a result, she became increasingly isolated and prone to self-harm, even as her songs were riding high on the charts. "I was so unhappy last year," she said in an interview, which aired as part of "The Gayle King Grammy Special." "I was so unhappy, and I was so joyless." She recalled contemplating suicide during a tour stop in Germany.

"I don't want to be too dark, but I genuinely didn't think I would make it to 17," said Eilish, who turned 18 in December. "I think about this one time I was in Berlin and I was alone in my hotel … And I remember there was a window right there … I remember crying because I was thinking about how the way that I was going to die was … I was going to do it."

She referenced her struggles in the song "Bury a Friend," which features the lyrics: "Today, I'm thinkin' about the things that are deadly, the way I'm drinkin' you down/Like I wanna drown, like I wanna end me."

There is another song that relays similar emotions: "Talkin' to myself and feelin' old/Sometimes I'd like to quit/Nothin' ever seems to fit/Hangin' around/Nothin' to do but frown," only these are not lyrics by Eilish. The lyrics to "Rainy Days and Mondays" were sung by another young female singer who, in 1970, was on a similar career trajectory, and was also overwhelmed by that success.

Nominated for the same awards as Eilish in 1970, Karen Carpenter won the GRAMMY for Best New Artist, an award she also shared with her brother Richard, her writing and performing partner in The Carpenters. Karen and Richard Carpenter can easily be viewed as the seminal sister/brother tandem that paved the way for Billie and Finneas. Much like Eilish, Karen Carpenter sang in a soft, hushed voice meant to draw you in, with her keyboard playing brother, Richard (in the pre-Finneas role), providing the melody for his sister to waft upon. Even the four-year age difference between Richard and Karen echoes that of Finneas and Billie. (Maybe the boys simply needed the head-start over their talented sisters?)

Insisting on becoming a drummer after bristling against being handed a glockenspiel in her high school band, Karen was initially nervous about performing in public, but said she "was too involved in the music to worry about it." In 1975, she was voted the best rock drummer in a poll of Playboy readers, beating Led Zeppelin's John Bonham. (No offense, but ...really?) Karen was a teenager, slightly older than Eilish, when she entered the Billboard charts, soon having her first #1 hit, "Close to You," right after her 20th birthday. Either solo or with her brother, Karen Carpenter's career resulted in 90 million albums sold and 32 various Top Ten Billboard hits.

12 years after that first #1 song, Karen Carpenter was dead, having passed away from anorexia nervosa, struggling with image and weight issues since high school. "How can anybody be too thin?" she once said, in a sad, but revealing moment. At one point in her battle, she weighed only 79 pounds.

"People never think of entertainers as being human," Carpenter said of the pressures of success and idolization. "When you walk out on stage, the audiences think, 'Nothing can go wrong with them.' We get sick and we have headaches just like they do. When we are cut, we bleed."

Eilish is no stranger to the criticism of her appearance. The negative comments and her own struggle with insecurities issues led Eilish to fixate on her self-image. She has been candid about the sometimes "toxic relationship" she has with her body, saying she has experienced periods of body dysmorphia, depression and self-harm over the years. She had naturally gravitated toward baggier clothes, which Eilish said has introduced problems as well.

"If I wore a dress to something, I would be hated for it. People would be like, 'You've changed, how dare you do what you've always rebelled against?' I'm like, 'I'm not rebelling against anything, really.' I can't stress it enough. I'm just wearing what I wanna wear. If there's a day when I'm like, 'You know what, I feel comfortable with my belly right now, and I wanna show my belly,' I should be allowed to do that. It's not that I like my body now. I just think I'm a bit more OK with it."

These days, the Los Angeles native finds herself in a much healthier state of mind and credits her mother, Maggie Baird, with convincing her not to end her own life, immediately scaling back her daughter's performance schedule and show business-related commitments to allow more time for self-care, a move that has clearly paid off.

Karen Carpenter's mother, Agnes, was the opposite of Maggie Baird. She was ashamed of her daughter's eating disorder. She felt that her daughter was "going overboard" with her dieting habits and never reached out to offer any real support. Karen Carpenter once said, "I may not be in control of anything else, but I am in control of my body." In the end, Karen lost that control, succumbing to years long abuse of laxatives, taking thyroid medicine to speed up her metabolism although she had no thyroid problems, and using ipecac syrup to induce vomiting. She had been eating, but also throwing it all up. Karen Carpenter had unknowingly dissolved her own heart muscle with the syrup.

Back in January, Billie shared a collection of photos on Instagram from a recent trip to Hawaii. The post included a shot of Billie in her bathing suit, and people had some things to say. "It was trending," Billie said. "There were comments like, 'I don't like her anymore because as soon as she turns 18, she's a whore.' Like, dude. I can't win. I can-not win."

On stage in Miami, Eilish addressed body-shaming and attempts to judge others for what they choose to wear: removing her t-shirt in the pre-recorded visual, she slowly sank into a pit of black tar before disappearing beneath the surface completely. "Some people hate what I wear; some people praise it; some people use it to shame others; some people use it to shame me," she says. "Would you like me to be smaller? Weaker? Softer? Taller? Would you like me to be quiet? Do my shoulders provoke you? Does my chest? Am I my stomach? My hips? The body I was born with — is it not what you wanted? If I wear what is comfortable, I am not a woman. If I shed the layers, I'm a slut. Though you've never seen my body, you still judge it and judge me for it. Why?"

It's been 50 years between Karen Carpenter's big win at the GRAMMY Awards and Billie Eilish's. Though neither Eilish, nor any of her fans, were even born when Karen Carpenter was alive, the two artists share an undeniable connection through the incredible pressures and unrelenting demands of success and the judgment of others. Eilish's experiences might suggest that not much has changed, but her actions prove otherwise. While Karen Carpenter's musical legacy can't help but be viewed from the shadows of her struggles, we can see hope that Eilish's future will move forward in the light. And with the continued support of her mother and brother, Eilish said she'd like to use her own experiences to pay it forward to her young fans, many of whom might be grappling with mental health concerns of their own. This was part of the reason for the video at the Miami concert.

Just before the GRAMMY winner for Album of the Year was announced, the 18-year-old Eilish could be seen at her seat mouthing, "Please don't be me," on camera. She then reacted by throwing her arms into the air and shouting "No" as her name was called for the award, against artists including Ariana Grande, who Eilish said should have won. She explains that this was a moment of humility, not self-shaming.

So, when we look for artists to stand up for themselves, and let their ravenous fans and critics know that their lives and their own well-being are not part of the deal, we can now look at Eilish and mouth, "Please be you."

DEAD ARE ALL THE GODS (PARTS 1 AND 2)

Right on, fight on…

Kenneth J. McKay

Originally Published Aug 4, 2020

Big Riffing

How Some Diminutive Musicians became Rock Giants

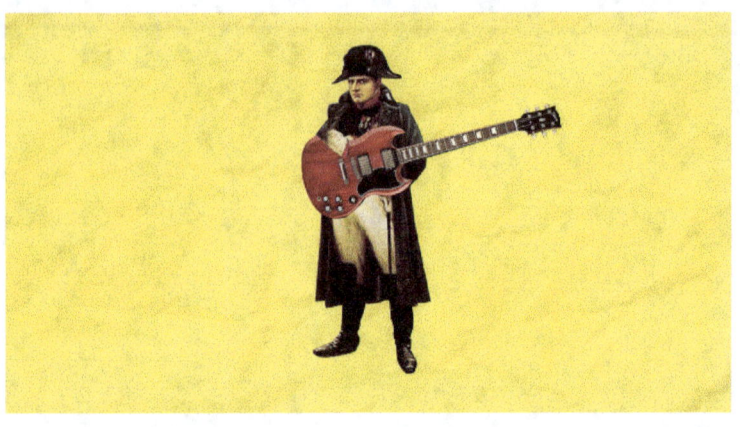

There was a book recently published about height discrimination titled, *Amazing Heights: How Short Guys Stand Tall*. This book notably mentions some familiar tech guys and should give some past, present, and future schoolyard bullies pause. The current richest man on the planet, Jeff Bezos, is 5'7". Zuckerberg is the same, but both are dwarfed by Google's Sergey Brin at a towering 5'8". (How long after I post this does my Internet crash?) This seems to fly in the face of some economists' theory of a "height premium" that translates into a 1.8-percent increase in wages that accompanies every additional inch of height. (Apparently, the inverse has been at work since the nerds took over.) Behavioral economist Dan Ariely found that for shorter men

113

to be judged attractive by American women, they must earn substantially more money than taller men. (Bezos recently hit $180 Billion…how tall, dark and handsome does that make a 5'7' bald man? …Shit, my Amazon Prime account just went down…WTF?)

Irish Poet Francis Duggan wrote of Death being the "Great Equalizer." Educational reformer Horace Mann felt that education was the great equalizer. Obviously, the authors of the book I just mentioned feel that brains are the platform shoes of Silicon Valley. But there is also a broad chorus (well, maybe me and a dude I used to know at Sam Goody's) who feel that music is the true great equalizer. I'm gonna run with this last one.

If you're simply a fan of good music, when you hear a song, your first thoughts are probably not concerned with what the sizes and shapes of the musicians are. You can't hear tall or skinny or short and wide. You just dig the tune. If you are a musician, when you hear somebody playing a great groove, you either want to sit back and take it in or jump up and jam with them. Again, it's the music that washes away all the other nonsense and brings us all into the fold. It's one big Seuss-ian chorus. No discrimination, no bullying, no bullshit. Music is magical that way.

40 years ago, on July 25th, the biggest selling Rock album of all time was released (no, not *Eagles—Their Greatest Hits (1971–1975)* …good Lord, these Eagles fans are exhausting). After finally hitting big with their most commercially successful album to date, *Highway to Hell*, AC/DC was poised to become one of the biggest acts on the planet, but in February of 1980, front man and lyricist Bon Scott died after sleeping off a drinking binge (the nod-nod, wink-wink way of politely saying he drowned in his own vomit). With international success now slipping from their reach, AC/DC did the impossible—replaced a seemingly irreplaceable part of the band and offered up a tribute to their lost mate in the form of the greatest comeback/reboot in Rock history. *Back in Black*, with 50 Million albums sales worldwide (best-selling Rock studio album to date), is arguably in the Top Ten Rock albums of all time, and the title track (which kicks off side 2) has as recognizable an opening riff as has ever been recorded (six guitar scratches, dropping out for two, leaving the hi-hat to lead us into…E (1x), D (3x), A (3x)…cool high string bluesy pull-off…E (1x), D(3x), A (3x)…awesome low string chromatic climb). So simple, so timeless. What guitar gods could have possibly pulled off a riff so massive, unleashed such a gargantuan guitar achievement of epic proportions? Well, it turns out it was actually a pair of somewhat vertically challenged Australian brothers. Malcolm and Angus Young

(5'3" and 5'2" respectively), and the dude charged with filling the huge shoes left behind by Bon Scott—Englishman Brian Johnson (all "chuffed" 5'5" of him) created a flawless album filled with one great rock tune after another. When this band steps on stage, they fill every corner of the venue with their sound, their energy and their very presence. True giants among men (well, musically, at least).

They say that on film the camera adds ten pounds to a person's appearance. If that holds true, then picking up a guitar easily adds ten feet to a person's height.

Well…kinda. How about…(ahem)…a tall tale?

Back in 1976, Aerosmith was also riding the crest of a wave after *Toys in the Attic* gave them a huge shot in the arm thanks to the killer-riff of "Walk this Way," a Top Ten hit for the band. In May of '76, they delivered *Rocks*, an album that shipped platinum. The diamonds on the front cover were a personal suggestion from guitarist Joe Perry (some silliness about diamonds being the hardest rocks and the album being the hardest rocking and a jewel in their catalog…this was right around his and Tyler's 'Toxic Twins' days), but it was the insert that really caught my eye. It was a really great illustration of the band by artist Teresa Stokes (an aviation artist, and yes that's a thing…they draw airplanes). It featured the band members on stage with Perry front and center.

What was truly cool was how she depicted his guitar and his hands being widely disproportionate to his body. He looked like he had massive hands playing a giant guitar. It really is a fantastic illustration. (Years later, Guitar Hero would depict him in a similar way in the video game.) After seeing Aerosmith at Madison Square Garden in support of Toys (back in the ancient days before giant live video screens), my only perspective was from Loge seats where every band member looked three inches tall anyway. There was no up-close-and-personal perspective, not even from the first row of orchestra seats. The larger-than-life notion was all you had to work with.

Then I saw Perry playing in a very small local club around 1984, after he had quit Aerosmith in 1979 (smooth move, Joe). The place was tight, with no real stage. I was right up front when the band came out, and I stayed there for the entire gig. That show left me with three impressions: 1) Joe was so stoned his eyes never opened during the set, 2) in spite of being so stoned, his guitar sound was amazing, and 3) Joe Perry is a tiny dude. That was the closest I had ever been to a major performer who I had previously only seen at Madison Square Garden from half-way up the arena, and the perspective hadn't changed much. I began to wonder how much of an exaggeration the Teresa Stokes illustration had been. (Was it the drug slouch, or the way he stands while playing? Dunno, but if you look at him in pics with other dudes, he's the chest high one.)

I had also seen the aforementioned AC/DC with Bon Scott when they opened for Rainbow at the Palladium in NYC. Angus was at his peak of running around on stage in a schoolboy uniform like a bad kid running from a teacher. Bon would put Angus up on his shoulders as he riffed out furiously to heighten the effect (no pun intended…sure). It was obvious that the band had a good sense of tongue in cheek about the whole thing and it just added to their anti-elite rockstar altitude (sorry, meant to say 'attitude').

Oddly enough, at that very same show, Rainbow was the headliner. This was also peak Rainbow, fronted by another colossal performer, Ronnie James Dio — the Stargazer who shouted from atop the Silver Mountain. All 5'4" of him. His voice was so powerful, he barely needed a microphone (add microphone stand jokes at your own risk…).

So, what is the point of all this, you might ask? (You may not have, but I'm going to tell you anyway.)

Long before the tech giants mentioned in the book took over the world and laughed in the face of heightism (they need a better name…this one just seems silly), musicians of all backgrounds figured out that music was one place where you could be whoever you were, or wanted to be, regardless of shape and size, and it's not just in Hard Rock. This list is deep, but here's a couple from the short list (couldn't help myself): Prince (5'3") proved his massive talent over a 40-year career as a writer, performer, and producer (as well as an excellent guitarist who could rock out when the mood hit. Just check out the George Harrison tribute at the 2004 Rock and Roll Hall of Fame show). Paul Simon (also 5'3") is possibly the greatest American composer of his generation. (I consider him to be the American Lennon/McCartney all by himself.) Genius knows no boundaries (horizontally or vertically). Billy Joel (5'5"), Phil Collins, (5' 6"), this list can go on for pages, but time is short… (insert groan here).

So, when researchers come up with their findings and bullies continue to be assholes and some people look down on others and up at money, they should look around for the short kid in the corner who just picked up a guitar and consider this: Sometimes, the yellow-brick road leads right to the Rock and Roll Hall of Fame. (Hmmm, what did Bernie Taupin (5'6") have in mind when he wrote that one for Elton John (5' 7")).

Rock on… (and stand tall)

Originally Published Sep 11, 2020

Love You Live

Why live Rock albums are a lost art and should be treasured

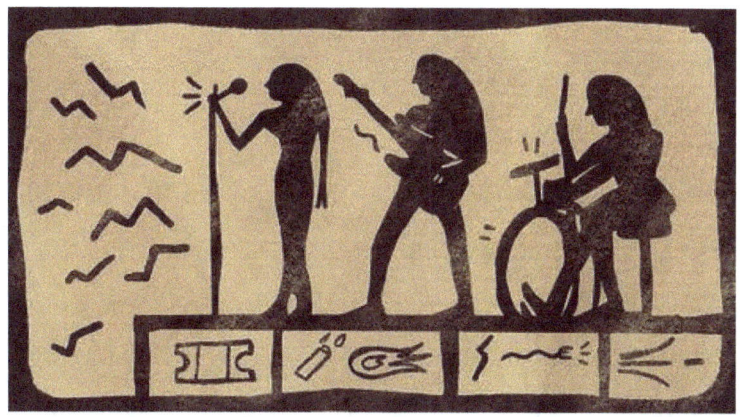

In 1976, an unusual phenomenon occurred that would shine a light on Rock artists in a way that had previously been reserved for die-hard fans and caused purists and critics alike to reconsider past opinions — a live album dominated the charts (reaching #1 and becoming the best-selling album of 1976) and changed the musical conversation for decades to come. The double live album, *Frampton Comes Alive!* was released to huge sales and quickly became the bible for generations of guitarists to come. That album, more than others who came before, brought a new legitimacy to live performances, as well as commercial viability to their recordings. It wasn't the first great live Rock album, but it was such a distinct piece of work that it could not be overlooked.

120

It was the perfect example of the live album as an art form. It wasn't just live versions of studio cuts; it was an expert offering of improvisation and re-imagining of studio songs. While some other live albums offered versions of songs that were already well known, *Frampton Comes Alive!* made hits out of songs that were not hits in their original incarnations. "Show Me the Way" and "Baby, I Love Your Way" (#6 and #12 on the Billboard Hot 100) were from his fourth studio album, Frampton, and "Do You Feel Like We Do" hit #10 on the same charts (after being edited from 14 minutes to 7 minutes — a previously unheard of running time for a single, never-mind a live recording...Okay, "Hey Jude" comes in at 7:11, but that was the Beatles. "In-A-Gadda-Da-Vida" was 2:52 as a single, before you chime in on that one.) "Baby, I Love Your Way" re-entered the charts in 1993 as a worldwide hit for the band Big Mountain.

The performances on the album transcended its vinyl restraints. "Do You Feel Like We Do" still gives chills after 40 years. The guitar work is literally stunning. Frampton's tone and dynamic control commanded guitarists' attention and is still marveled at to this day. The nuance-filled intro to this song is one of the most recognizable pieces of fret play to come out of the 70s (and is a great way to scratch a guitar itch when you're just fumbling around for something to play), the solos are a master class in the use of the Dorian scale (uh, mode!…damn purists), and the legendary talk-box interlude is, well, legendary. Even the modified three-pick-up 1954 Les Paul Custom has a mythical back story all its own.

Again, to the artistry of the album, it's not just about Frampton. The album showcases what great journeymen musicians can add. The late great Bob Mayo handles so many subtle tasks, from the second guitar harmonies on "DYFLWD" to the Fender Rhodes soloing that so perfectly matched Frampton's solos on that same song just a few minutes later, that he may have just been the alchemist that made the album truly come alive. Even the drum intro to "(I'll Give You) Money" elevated John Siomos from a relative unknown to "that guy" (oddly reminiscent of "I'm Ready" from Humble Pie's *Performance Rockin' the Fillmore*, Frampton's last performance before leaving that band).

So, what was so special about this album, or any live album? Live recordings allow an artist to show that they are more than the confines of a studio and a producer, that they are more than a record company's pre-packaged product. They prove, in a way, that musicians are actually living people, and equally important, that music is a living entity that changes and grows with the audience experiencing it.

In the world of Rock emerging in the 1970s, live performances were becoming the thing of legend. The Monterey International Pop Music Festival in 1967 and Woodstock two years later had proven that audiences were drawn to the live music experience in massive numbers. Unfortunately, the soundtracks to these specific events didn't truly live up to the experiences themselves. They were recordings of live events, but they weren't expressly "live" albums. They offered some amazing moments from a huge selection of the most important artists of the day, but those albums seemed to miss the intimacy of some of the truly great live albums by individual artists. Jimi Hendrix is the lone exception. His immortal version of "The Star-Spangled Banner" at Woodstock and his killer performance of "Wild Thing" (where he literally killed his guitar) at Monterey might be the standout performances of both concerts and represent the best of live Hendrix. (*Band of Gypsys*, recorded at the Fillmore East without his original band, was produced to settle a contract dispute. The duress kinda bleeds through the performance. Just sayin'...)

The Who's performance at both of these festivals just doesn't compare to their *Live at Leeds* album — "the definitive hard-rock holocaust" (New York Times review...NYT...really?). *Live at Leeds* has been cited as the best live rock recording of all time by multiple outlets, including Rolling Stone, and critics' have said, "Few bands ever moved a mountain of sound around with this much dexterity and power," and upon the reissue of the album that includes additional content from a second performance, "we now have the two greatest live rock albums…ever."

Live albums were becoming unique unto their own selves.

If there was one figure who could be singled out as the biggest influence on great live performances, thereby paving the way to great live albums, it was Bill Graham.

Graham's Fillmore venues (East and West) were the backdrop for some of the greatest live albums recorded. The list is long for the Fillmore shows, (Grateful Dead, Miles Davis, Jimi Hendrix, Johnny Winter, and on and on), but for live albums, the following two always seemed to emerge as timeless:

The Allman Brothers Band — At Fillmore East. "Whipping Post", "Hot 'Lanta", "In Memory of Elizabeth Reed". Every track is priceless. (Could you even imagine not having this album to immortalize Duane Allman?) This album just confirmed what every Allman Bros. fan already knew — this was a band to be experienced live. The studio albums were great, but merely a formality. This album is in the Library of Congress and is listed in the top 50 of Rolling Stone's 500 greatest albums of all time, and was named by one critic, "the finest live rock performance ever committed to vinyl."

Humble Pie — Performance Rockin' the Fillmore. The precursor to Frampton's huge live album is his last performance before leaving the band. The drum opener for "Are You Ready", Steve Marriott's vocal riffing during "Stone Cold Fever", and every garage band's jammer, "I Don't Need No Doctor" are classics across the board.

Parts of Frampton's album were recorded at another Graham venue — Winterland Ballroom (an old ice-skating rink, of all things) in San Francisco. Three of the four live parts of Cream's Wheels of Fire were recorded there. Though technically not a full live album, where would guitar rock (or Clapton) be if not for the version of "Crossroads" that was committed to legend that night?

Another arena which seemed to offer up timeless live recordings was Cobo Hall in Detroit. Literally everybody who was anybody played this arena at its peak: Zeppelin, Sabbath, The Who, The Stones, Hendrix, The Doors...everybody...but certain live recordings captured a few performances that resonated more than the others.

From his home base of Detroit, Bob Seger's Live Bullet hit the mark dead on. It was his breakout moment. The album is over 5x Platinum and still selling, adding to his eventual career sales of over 75 million, induction into the Songwriters Hall of Fame and the Rock and Roll Hall of Fame. The live "Turn the Page" is classic (and another example of a better version of a studio tune) and you could almost put a pin in that live recording as the beginning of his success.

Cobo Hall also gave us what just might be the most controversial live album ever recorded, *KISS Alive!* Partially recorded at Cobo Hall and several other stops on their Dressed to Kill tour in 1975, *KISS Alive!* was released in 1975 to great success. It charted as high as #9, ultimately staying on the charts for over 100 weeks. Prior to the live album, KISS's three studio albums were commercial disappointments, and even though they were generating a cult following for their stage performances, their power was undoubtedly their onstage visual element. (I saw them in NYC in 1975 and it remains one of the most memorable shows I have ever attended. I was 12 years old…maybe that should factor in.) Capturing a spectacle is different than recording a great live album. Enter the controversy (here's where Gene Simmons sues me). As the buzz around the album was peaking, people began to accuse the band of re-recording and overdubbing tracks and even adding pre-recorded audience sounds. In his 2001 autobiography, Gene Simmons said, "There have always been rumors that the *Alive!* record was substantially reworked in the studio. It's not true … what we wanted, and what we got, was proof of the band's rawness and power." Two years later, the band's founders owned up. Paul Stanley admitted, "What we felt was necessary was to capture the energy of the performance, not necessarily having it note for note of what actually happened." Simmons said: "Most people assume it was all live, it wasn't." Regardless of the controversy, Guitar World magazine ranks it at #3 on its greatest live albums list. So, Audiens Cave…listener beware.

Another band whose recognition was unquestionably elevated by a live album was The J. Geils Band, a bluesy bar band out of the Boston/Worcester area that started getting some noteworthy opening act gigs in 1970 but couldn't yet get to top billing. They released two modestly received studio albums that didn't really capture where the band truly shined — in live performances. In 1972, they released *"Live" Full House,* and everything changed. The album became their first gold record, and their next studio album, *Bloodshot*, hit #10 on the Billboard 200. *Full House* notably showcased an evolution of harmonica in rock music. Magic Dick's performance on "Whammer Jammer" rivaled anything a guitar player had done live up to that point, and it stands out even to this day, but it was Peter Wolf's boundless energy and dynamism as a front man that made the band's live shows legendary. His intro to "Musta Got Lost" on their second live album, *Blow Your Face Out*, (a double album also partially recorded at Cobo) is a two-minute-long master class in how to make a giant arena seem as intimate as a local bar.

RUSH has released multiple live albums, each one a relevant snapshot of their long progression as a band at the time of the release, but 1976's *All the World's a Stage*, their first live album (released to buy some time in between studio albums) put the power of the Canadian trio on full display and made the music world aware of what Neil Peart was unleashing upon the world of modern rock drummers (Long Live the Professor). It became their first Top 40 album and went gold and eventually platinum. Again, a double-live album breaking the Top 40.

Deep Purple's *Made in Japan* is a live tour de force. An unapologetically hard-driving, powerful showcase of each member's command of their instruments, *Made in Japan* is a double live masterpiece that predates Frampton's success by three years. The album went platinum within a month of release. Though not a singles driven band, they had a surprising hit with the studio version of "Smoke on the Water" as they were performing the song live on tour. The studio cut hit #4 in the U.S. with the live version as a B-side to the 45. Though "Smoke" became a concert staple for decades after, it's the live "Highway Star" that really stands out on the album. (Crank it up, fuck the speed limit, take your chances.) *Made in Japan* sits at #6 on Rolling Stone's best live album list (every once in a while, they get things right). Great album.

Another Japanese success story for live albums was 1979's *Cheap Trick at Budokan*. Cheap Trick had failed to chart any singles as of their second album, but on the strength of a rabid fan base in Japan, they recorded the shows during their 1978 tour there with the intent of releasing a live album in Japan only. They released their third studio album, *Heaven Tonight*, and scored a moderately charting single with, "Surrender". Epic Records responded by releasing *Cheap Trick at Budokan*, which quickly went triple platinum and made a #7 hit single out of the previously ignored, "I Want You to Want Me". Live luck strikes again.

Back to Clapton, his *Unplugged* album is by far his best selling (26 million sold) and also featured a re-imagined version of his most popular song, "Layla", but this is where I begin to get a little particular about this topic. Yes, this is a "live" album, but its origin is in the well-planned, pre-packaged and thoughtfully produced concept of MTV's Unplugged series. It is as close to a studio production as a live album can be. It captures a studio-like performance with a carefully curated audience. Yes, it has some surprise highlights (like "Layla"), yet it lacks the spontaneity that truly great live albums provide. It just seems like a performance you would expect from Clapton at that point in his career. It was designed to succeed.

Now, to contradict what I just said, *MTV Unplugged in New York* by Nirvana came two years after Clapton's mega-selling album turned the Unplugged concept and brand into an industry unto itself. Though rehearsed heavily and recorded with a full production team in Sony Studios, the performance managed to ignore all the hype and offer a side to Cobain that was so intimate, powerful and revelatory that its value as a live statement shouldn't be overshadowed by the money machine that was behind its design. Kurt Cobain gave one of the most honest and soul baring performances on record. The album debuted at #1, being released five months after Cobain's death, and went on to double-digit platinum sales. The critical reception was fawning, and the album is #1 or close to it on just about every top live album list.

An interesting live album that crossed over to the Billboard 200 was *Johnny Cash at Folsom Prison*, a live album recorded in a prison (talk about a captive audience! Sorry, I had to say it). The album revitalized Cash's career at that point (one of many comebacks), hitting #1 on Country charts and #13 on Pop charts, ultimately becoming triple platinum over its lifetime release, and its success predictably led to three subsequent live albums recorded in various prisons. (Was it a live Rock album? No. It was Johnny Cash. Enough said.)

So, for those of you wondering (or expressing some form of outrage), *The Last Waltz* or *The Song Remains the Same* are not going to get the same consideration as other albums mentioned here. These albums are soundtracks that accompany films.

The Last Waltz was explicitly developed as a screen project by Robbie Robertson and Martin Scorsese. It is probably the greatest concert movie ever, but that's where it lives. It's filled with legendary guest artists and retrospective interviews that highlight The Band's impact and influence. The performances are fantastic, it is a true moment in Rock history, but its life is on film. If you need to experience *The Last Waltz*, watch it, don't simply listen to it.

The Song Remains the Same is a similar case. Yes, it is a live performance and everything Zeppelin did live was a departure from their studio recordings, but this was still conceived as a film performance and will be treated as such. Oddly enough, the footage for this film was from Madison

Square Garden, a venue that is historic for its concerts, yet has yielded few great live albums.

Ok, I know you've been waiting...The Grateful Dead. The Grateful Dead might have the largest volume of live recordings floating around the ether just through the sheer dedication of their traveling fan base (second only to the annual Serengeti migration). Officially, *Live/Dead* is their first live album, but from that point until this very day, the number of live performances committed to tape, vinyl, cd, digital media (and weed-fueled gray matter) are impossible to count. So, for Deadheads, you know your favorite live performance, you don't need me.

The great live album is lightning in a bottle. It is fresh every time you listen to it. It is timeless and it allows artists to live on forever. It allows us to return to a time in our lives (ahem...our youth) when that moment was all there was, especially for anyone lucky enough to have been at the show that was recorded. Modern technology may have incidentally robbed us of great live albums by allowing groups to replicate exact renditions of studio recordings, eliminating that tightrope prospect that anything might happen. Improvisation (and even the inevitable mistake) gives birth and rebirth to new and old music alike. It is in those dangerous moments where things don't sound "just like the record" that gifted artists either sink or swim. They turn unexpected live moments into legendary ones.

Rock on...Live.

DEAD ARE ALL THE GODS (PARTS 1 AND 2)

Originally Published Mar 6, 2021

Shut Up and Play

When instrumentals speak louder than words

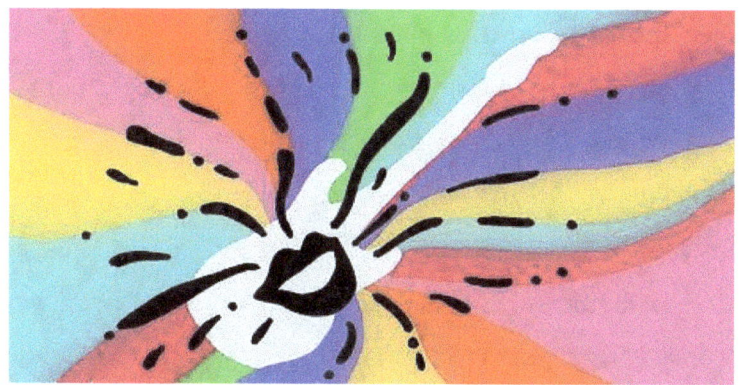

"Music and Lyrics by..." are the standard credits by which songwriters make a living. When both of these are good, they can make a good song into a great song. When they're both great, then you have something memorable. But what happens when words just seem to get in the way? You end up with some of the greatest examples of musical expression: instrumentals. Instrumentals have been around forever: in classical music, in jazz, in roots music, but once Rock and Roll musicians started to exercise their opinions in the genre, well...things got real...and loud. Now, I know (and agree) that the voice is an instrument, and there is an entire genre of vocal instrumentals provided by some very unique a cappella groups, with the earlier and more notable Doo-Wop groups

134

of the 1950s and early '60s, such as The Cadillacs, The Coasters, and Little Anthony and the Imperials in the vanguard. A Cappella groups have also had a renaissance in the current scene with standouts like Pentatonix, and have even spawned films like Pitch Perfect to celebrate the genre. That the voice is an instrument is acknowledged here, but for the purposes of this rant, I'm sticking to the other side of the stage: the musicians. More to the point: the guitar players. Instrumentals started popping onto the charts as early as 1957 with the #3 hit "Raunchy" by Bill Justis, then a #1 topper with "Tequila" by The Champs, but some of these early examples were almost a kind of jam sessions in blues progressions, like "Honky Tonk" by Bill Doggett, or country-tinged pieces, like "Rebel-'Rouser" by Duane Eddy. Things could also get cool, like "Rumble" by Link Wray. (The "Theme from Peter Gunn" is one of the earliest "cool" riffs you can learn on the guitar, but Henry Mancini ain't getting on this list, even if Duane Eddy did bring it some Rock credibility a year later.) The first song to inspire air-drumming, "Wipeout" charted at #3 in 1963. (Oddly enough, "Green Onions" charted at #1 on the R&B charts, not the Rock chart...) This was all good and worthwhile music, but then, in the latter part of the '60s, guitar-centric instrumentals began to take shape, becoming more than what had almost been an excuse to trade solos or jump on a trend.

(Dick Dale did give a bit of a heads-up for what might happen when guitarists took the helm, with his surf version of "Misirlou." We were all reminded of this once again when Tarantino featured it in *Pulp Fiction* thirty years later.) Jeff Beck (of course), alluding to what he would eventually be capable of, dropped "Beck's Bolero" on the unsuspecting world, and people took notice. A year later, Peter Green's brilliant "Albatross," showed the audience why a well-played guitar can be as expressive as the greatest of vocal offerings (and gave cred to Fleetwood Mac...which they would later surrender to Stevie Nicks). In 1970, Carlos Santana released his second album, *Abraxas*, which ended up charting at #1 on the strength of songs like "Black Magic Woman" and "Oye Como Va", both covers of earlier hits by other composers (the aforementioned Peter Green and Tito Puente, respectively), but it was the original instrumental composition, "Samba Pa Ti" that demonstrated Santana's incredibly emotional guitar playing. This was no raw musical jam like "Soul Sacrifice" from his first album. It was a beautifully constructed piece that foreshadowed a career full of amazing instrumentals, like the 1976 masterpiece, "Europa". 1970 also saw the release of *Idlewild South*, another sophomore effort, this time from the Allman Brothers Band. This album contained "In Memory of Elizabeth Reed," a Dickie Betts-penned instrumental of which Rolling Stone originally said the song "just goes and goes for a stupendous, and unnoticed, seven minutes." The live version that followed a year later on the timeless *At Fillmore East*, highlighted not only Betts and Duane Allman's transcendent guitar playing, but the virtuosity of the entire band and remains considered the definitive version. (It would be a huge oversight not to mention "Hot 'Lanta" here as well). Betts later followed this up with the more upbeat and equally identifiable "Jessica" from *Brothers and Sisters*. Among the more unique instrumentals to pop up in 1970 was a classic from the inimitable Frank Zappa. His "Peaches en Regalia" evoked so much imagery from Zappa's seemingly endless musical imagination and inventive instrumentation that you couldn't be sure if it was meant for the listener or if you were somehow eavesdropping on a group of musicians-on-the-run-hiding-in-a-traveling-circus jamming after hours under the big top. Complex and fun at the same time, the song is pure musical brilliance. All these great instrumentals were sitting there beside the singles on high-charting albums, but how far could the idea of Rock-ready instrumentals go as far as bankability on their own merits? Well, released in 1973, "Frankenstein" by the Edgar Winter Group was a monster #1 hit (couldn't help myself…but you were thinking it too) selling over a million copies, and had everything a hard-rocking music fan could ask for — great guitar work from the late Ronnie Montrose, seemingly unheard-of awesome keyboard sounds, a drum solo (with kettle drums thrown in for good measure!) — it truly ran the gamut. With record companies clearly caught flat-footed by the success of "Frankenstein," Sire records released the instrumental single, "Hocus Pocus" by the Dutch band, Focus, in the summer of 1973. "Hocus Pocus" had been from the band's 1971 album, *Focus II*, but didn't generate any radio play until it hit the UK airwaves in early 1973. Was it the success of "Frankenstein" that led to "Hocus Pocus" charting as high as #9 in the U.S. two years after its original album appearance? Who knows, but the song is a Rock-lover's dream with fantastic fretwork by Jan Akkerman, "Frankenstein"-esque drum solos and other fantastical interludes (the flutes were acceptable, but yodeling? seriously? Whatever…it worked). So, by 1973, instrumental Rock singles proved to be commercially viable. But then what? Jeff Beck is what (of course). In 1975, Jeff Beck turned his attention back to instrumentals. After four albums of varied versions of a group, Jeff released the solo album, *Blow by Blow*, an entirely instrumental masterpiece produced by none other than George Martin (yes, that George Martin) that charted at #4 and was ultimately certified platinum. Close your eyes and drop your finger anywhere on the track list and you will land on musical genius. "'Cause We've Ended as Lovers," written by Stevie Wonder (supposedly returning the favor for Beck's involvement in Wonder's massive hit "Superstition") might just be the pinnacle that all others since have been trying to reach. A year later, Beck followed this up with *Wired*. Producing a back-to-back triumph of instrumental music that so few could hope for, Wired hit #16 on the charts, went platinum, and cemented Jeff Beck in his place as the standard for any guitarists hoping to use their instrument to speak for them (Beck is the standard for so many guitar-related things, this one doesn't surprise, or end the still evolving list). The ability to influence generations to come is the true sign of greatness versus fads. Was it Jeff Beck's groundbreaking work that encouraged someone with the vocal power of Stevie Ray Vaughan to let his guitar do the talking on the instrumental piece "Lenny" from his debut album? Probably, but whatever the case, "Lenny" is so distinctively SRV that his choice to let that specific '65 Strat say it all was pure luck on our part. (He later used it on "Riviera Paradise" and almost religiously only used that guitar to play "Lenny" live. (Note: In my opinion, the posthumously released SRV instrumental version of "Little Wing" is second only to the original, and since this is my post, well, my opinion kinda overrules any other...just sayin'.) Do we get a Joe Satriani without a Jeff Beck? Possibly, but Joe's entrance and acceptance was undoubtedly made easier by Jeff's paving of the way. Satriani's virtuosity became evident so quickly that it was no surprise that his second album *Surfing with the Alien* remained on the Billboard 200 charts for 75 weeks and eventually went platinum and was nominated for the Best Rock Instrumental Performance at the 1989 Grammy Awards. (By the way, what's with all these "sophomore" albums turning up in this post? Were they saving the good stuff just in case? Who knows, but, hey…who cares? They did it, we got it. What else matters?) We definitely can say that without Joe Satriani, we might not have Steve Vai, another instrumentalist extraordinaire. Joe was his guitar teacher (Steve later joined Frank Zappa's band), along with many other students/future guitar heroes, including Andy Timmons, whose "Cry for You" is an absolute must listen. (Go listen to it now…I can wait…6:55 passes…TOLD YA SO! Amazing.) The 1990s did not disappoint as "Cliffs of Dover" from Eric Johnson's Ah Via Musicom, blew guitar players' minds with Johnson's perfect tone and mind-bending harmonics and went on to win a Grammy Award for Best Rock Instrumental Performance (beating out RUSH…read on). Rock instrumentals have always found their way into the set lists of some of the greatest bands in history, but one band in particular could always be counted on to deliver the goods album after album — RUSH. The 2112 "Overture" flipped the musical bird at critics and defined the band at their most experimental. Then, in 1978, "La Villa Strangiato" put the trio's unquestionable mastery of their instruments on full display with perfectly executed solos and time changes that knotted unsuspecting guitar and bass players' fingers while causing even braver drummers to just toss their sticks into the air in exasperation (don't try this one at home kids). Then, in 1981, came their first Grammy nod for the "YYZ". More concise than "La Villa," this tune packed all the punch into tight sequences and solos (check out the RUSH in Rio live version to hear the audience of 40,000 "sing" along to the melody). RUSH went on to garner six Grammy nods for Best Rock Instrumental Performance. (They should have won every single time, but they always had to skirt the haters and forge their own path, so fuck the Grammys.) Ok, so back to 'Overtures.' I included the 2112 "Overture" because it kinda steps outside the traditional overture concept. Yes, it somewhat represents the whole theme of the piece, but it has truly come to stand on its own. You could effectively stop right before "The Temples of Syrinx " and it works. Now with "Overture" from *Tommy*, that piece truly foreshadows the entire album that follows, so yes, it's great, but it's not really presented as an instrumental. That being said, "Sparks" from the same album is a great track that gave even more as a live performance, unleashing a live Keith Moon (as if was ever leashed). Soooo, the elephant in the room... "Eruption." "Eruption" changed the world of

141

guitar players forever. It's 1:42 of history in the making. Is it "instrumental"? Obviously. Is it instrumental? No. "Eruption" is a guitar solo that no song could possibly contain. It became the intro to "You Really Got Me" to the benefit of that song. Though Van Halen gives some nods to Page's "Heartbreaker" solo after seeing it performed live in L.A. (he acknowledges Page's one-handed pulls inspired his experimentation into what became his own legendary technique), "Eruption" took stand-alone soloing to an unprecedented level. It was Eddie's debut moment, and to insert it into a song (à la "Heartbreaker") would have been an injustice, especially a song that was written by someone else. So, a great "instrumental" piece of guitar work — unquestionable, but a great instrumental — no (with the stated caveat in place). The same goes for a song like "Moby Dick." This piece was really just an excuse for a solo, this time a drum solo (kinda seemed like a "tit-for-tat" with "Heartbreaker" on the same album). Now, this post could clearly go on for multiple pages filled with endless examples, but time is precious, so go find some on your own. They're out there. And don't hold any of this against the great singers who fronted some of these bands, but sometimes you have just bench them and let the music do the talking (unless you're Steven Tyler who just had to sing the lyrics for Aerosmith's ironically titled "Let the Music Do the Talking."

50 years, 15 albums, more than 100+ tunes and one 3:44 minute Brad Whitford instrumental throwaway on a compilation album... really?).

Shut up and Rock On.

<u>Afterword</u>

In an effort to make the original essay a more concise read (a 1500 word post is considered ideal), I split it into two parts (but still blew past the acceptable limit on both parts...oh,well). I put all the guitar-centric stuff into Part 2 and have included it here for the guitar freaks, geeks, and nerds.

You're welcome.

Originally Published Dec 27, 2018

Dead Are All the Gods (Part Two)

Part 2: The Four Horsemen of the Apocalypse of Guitar Goddery

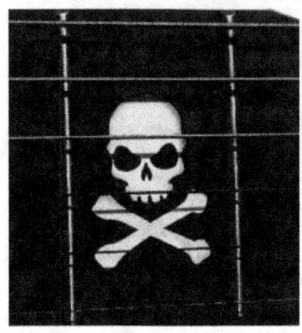

I have seen the Four Horsemen of the Apocalypse of Guitar Goddery (just consider that phrase copyrighted) and they ain't pretty (for creative purposes, we'll stick to just four).

Horseman #1: The Chibson

No, not a band, an instrument (Chinese Gibson knock-offs, come on, so obvious).

There's currently an endless supply of these instruments on eBay. While a couple of knockoffs floating around on the internet is to be expected, this is something different. These guitars look identical to Gibsons, and it's not just Les Pauls; it's 335s, SGs, Juniors - the whole freaking Gibson catalog. Again, not a game changer, but...these guitars have serial numbers and "Made in USA " stamped into the back of the headstocks on the obverse of a picture-perfect Gibson logo.

This big push on eBay coincides directly (or so it would seem) with Gibson's recent bankruptcy filing (and as I Google the specifics of the filing, an ad pops up for the very eBay Chibsons I mentioned. Un-fucking-real) and amid countless threads online about a decline in Gibson's quality standards (not to mention that Gibson knocks off themselves with redundant models under the Epiphone name. Why spend over $3000 on a Gibson when the identical (looking) guitar is literally on the next rack for less than half the price?). When I first started playing (then collecting, because that's how the vicious cycle starts. You have to have a back-up for each guitar you're using at a gig, so if you have one Strat, you need a second, and so on and so on). It mattered that you had a "real" guitar, and that meant a Fender or a Gibson. The early days of Ibanez and Yamaha weren't getting any respect and those "lawsuit" Tokais and Grecos were persona non-grata, though they get unbelievable prices on the resale market now. They're as collectible as anything else from the late 60s and 70s. Go figure. Billy Gibbons, who reveres his 1959 "Pearly Gates" Les Paul burst, has often played a freakin' Tokai on stage. And, as I mentioned previously, there's Slash's Derrig copy.

Now, Strats have been getting knocked off for years, essentially because you could take them apart and put them back together so easily. They pretty much lent themselves to the idea of customization and modification. (Blackmore was the first I heard of - gluing the neck to the body, killing the middle position pick-up and wiring the others out of phase. You can hear it actually. He sounds different from other Strat players of his time.) Removable pickguards with the pick-ups and wiring all onboard; fully exposed wiring troughs in the body; and bolt-on necks were the key to the tomfoolery. You could essentially gouge out the body and stick all kinds of shit in there. There are a multitude of nightmare mods hiding under pickguards all across the guitar playing world (oy vey). Even high-profile players like Clapton and Gilmore were swapping parts between different Strats they owned, seeking that sweet spot of comfort and tone. As the legend goes, in 1970, Clapton bought six 50's era Strats. He gave away three - to Harrison, Townshend and Winwood-then took the best parts of the other three to make his well-known "Blackie" guitar (which was bought by Guitar Center in 2004 for $850,000 and is now on display at their Times Square location).

Fender has allegedly sued several aftermarket suppliers through the years, like Mighty Mite, but tough turds. Then Van Halen did what he did with whatever the Hell that was he was playing and Fender didn't know what hit 'em.

Non-Fender Strat-like guitars were everywhere. They may also have been the first to bogart their own stuff with the Squier line, the occasional Japan-made guitars, and ultimately the MIM models. Nevertheless, Fender is hanging in there (they hold a small edge over Gibson in market share), but both manufacturers are carrying huge debt loads, as is Paul Reed Smith.

Gibson's inherent design and construction may have helped them push back against any blatant attempts at total knockoffs (for a while, at least). The set necks stalled any real tear down of the guitar. You got what you got. The wiring channels were buried inside the body and harnesses were cumbersome to remove. Some bolder players sanded the necks for more desirable profiles and tinkered with the pots (Page has some out of phase, push/pull mod going on in Number One); some changed tuners and nuts; but until Seymour Duncan came along with pick-up options, nobody really changed the true nature of a Les Paul.

Then came the sleeping dragon! (hat tip to Napoleon).

China figured it out. It's that simple. Cheap labor, low material costs, no restrictive environmental policies. Chop down some trees, ignore all the IP, and crank out the gee-tars. The first years of stuff from China was obvious garbage, but once they got their hands on true production specs (provided by Gibson themselves in the factories they set up - the Epiphone gambit), it was a "one for you, two for me" scenario gone wild (just like sneakers, but with a better margin). People are talking about how the Chibson quality has jumped (single piece wood bodies, better nuts, better fret work, decent to good pick-ups) as Gibson quality has reportedly receded (other people's opinions, not mine...uh-hem).

Horseman #2: **The Ghost**

(Derived from the Millennial: Ghosting (noun) informal -the practice of suddenly ending all contact with a person without explanation, especially in a romantic relationship.)

A recent concert of absolute guitar virtuosos and general six-string lunatics dubbed *Generation Axe - A Night of Guitars* played at the well-known venue, the Capitol Theater (capacity 1800). This show consisted of none other than Steve Vai, Zakk Wylde, Yngwie Malmsteen, Nuno Bettencourt, and the interesting addition of Tosin Abasi. Five very different dudes who can each play like there's no tomorrow. The show was on a Wednesday and the weather was ok, yet...there were still tickets available as of showtime! (Look at that line-up one more time...and, not sold out immediately. WTF?) In full disclosure, I did not go either (fucking phony, preachy asshat!) I just couldn't get there (yea, sure), but I was literally checking the website right up until the final cutoff. I had seen Zakk Wylde doing his Zakk Sabbath show this time last year at the Chance in Poughkeepsie (capacity 900), and then saw Malmsteen at the Paramount in Peekskill (capacity 1025) after that.

The Zakk Sabbath show was incredible. Packed, but we're talking less than 1000 people. It's Zakk Wylde, for crying out loud. A sell-out should be expected, but tickets were pretty easy to come by.

Then came the Malmsteen fiasco. This place was so empty, it was practically hollow. I remember standing in line for the Men's room at Hammerheads during a Zebra gig with more people. This guy literally had dozens of Marshall stacks walled across the back of the stage (it almost felt like there was one for every person in the orchestra). You could feel the uneasiness at the soundboard.

That probably had something to do with my apprehension about going over to the Capitol for the *Generation Axe* show. It's all about perception. If nobody else is going, why bother? (That's some stupid thinking right there...I know). Even though I'm not a real follower, I have never seen Steve Vai, and I probably (no, definitely) should (though I still can't get past the ridiculous Ralph Macchio guitar battle in that Crossroads movie). Like him or not, the guy is one of the premier guitarists of all time. But this seems to be the way things are going for these players these days. I saw Satriani at the Capitol, and also at Webster Hall with Chickenfoot. Both of these shows were full, but if this was 30 years ago, Chickenfoot would have sold out Madison Square Garden, they're just that kind of band. Marquee names, good songs, great players.

I'm sure people can find ways to call "bullshit" on this by citing things like the GnR reunion tour, Aerosmith's upcoming Social Security gigs in Vegas (oh, that's not what their residency out there is called? It should be. Joe Perry is having more heart attacks on stage than Steven Tyler has fallen off of lately. And this is coming from someone who loves Aerosmith and had seen them on their first "Toys" gig at MSG, and then when they headlined at the Meadowlands…and got dusted by GnR. Sorry, that gig was historic for Axl and the band). Anyways, those big summer tours are all fueled by nostalgia, not new music. KISS just announced a farewell tour (again) that will last three years. Gene Simmons will be 72 by the time the tour ends. (Do we really need to see a man in his seventies dressed in makeup and costumes?) In 2014, Robert Plant supposedly nixed an 800 million dollar offer from Richard Branson for a Led Zeppelin reunion tour. (Thank God. Finally, someone who gets it. Plant, not Branson.) The only band who still seemed to tour off of new music (and what great music!) was RUSH, and they also realized that touring just to tour wasn't sustainable anymore, even though they consistently filled arenas and large venues worldwide. Neil understood the toll it was taking on him physically and that it would ultimately become harder to play to the exacting standards of the music. Here's where we simply thank them for the decades of phenomenal music and respect their decision. Hat's off to one of the greatest bands in rock history (and the best Hall of Fame acceptance speech ever). From the A-list, The Rolling Stones are planning another world tour; Paul (no last name required) is actually out promoting a bunch of new tunes (wait, I thought you just said no new music…? (insert eye roll). He's a Beatle. He can do whatever he wants.); Ringo will undoubtedly head out with the All-Stars (again, a Beatle); U2 will probably bore (I mean, bless) us with another extravaganza of relentless relevance. The B-list is finite and predictable (insert every 70s era band that still has at least one original member and/or has replaced former members with someone they found on YouTube).

There is good reason for these romps through our misspent (and long lost) youth. These bands can make significantly more money touring now than they ever did in their past histories, and why not, the music holds up (even when the players don't). There were some very high-grossing tours from these bands, but they were severely outpaced by the neo-popstars, and let's not kid ourselves here, people of the 60s and 70s generations are out there for these bigger bands because they have the cash and it's unfortunately a bit of an unspoken death watch (on both sides of the show). Just a quick glance at the loss of the major and minor musical giants of our day due to time and tides is enough to make you look hard in the mirror (and check under your armpits). The foolishly romanticized and morosely legendary senseless airplane crashes, overdoses, and motorcycle accidents have been replaced with the diseases of mere mortals: heart attacks, cancer and suicide (this last one is truly the saddest. What world is better off without Keith Emerson or Butch Trucks? I don't know one...so sad). So, yeah, people will shell out large for a "final" tour, but it's the guys in the trenches that need us to show up. Freaking Zakk Wylde has got to be the hardest working dude I have ever seen live. He played his ass off, non-stop - singing, killing the long solos - just a real blue-collar working musician doing it for us, except when we ain't there. I'm ashamed. Next time, I'm there, brother.

<u>Horseman #3:</u> The Stone

As the saying goes, "a rolling stone gathers no moss", that stone will sooner or later stop rolling, and when it does, it might need to get out of the road.

There was a time when "Rock Star" actually meant someone who played rock and roll with an attitude and didn't give a shit who cared. Then along came a self-appointed, so-called "Hall of Fame" and things started to get muddy (God, I love when I drop a bunch of inside references that only me and… well, probably only me…will get). Anyway, the Rock and Roll Hall of Fame started a stone rolling down a path that wasn't particularly straight. Lines didn't become blurred; they were intentionally smudged for reasons that people felt were personal and/or musically political. There can be any number of Halls of Fame for each and every person who wants to have one, but when you call yours the "Rock and Roll" Hall, it would be best if you respected the genre, the players, and the fans who made it what it is and what it should never be. Now, this is not a slight to any of the musicians, songwriters or performers who had no input into their being nominated (ergo, dragged into this mess) and/or indicted (oops…inducted) into this "Hall of Fame", but in what world is ABBA (2010) inducted into anything preceded by the words "rock and roll" before Deep Purple (2016). I know "Waterloo" is a catchy tune, but how many young guitarists sat on the edge of their beds banging that out on some shitty, borrowed, six-stringed, plywood-bodied turd of a guitar with action so bad your fingers bled? No way, you dancing queens, that tune was "Smoke on the Water", and it was worth every ounce of blood and knuckle to bungle that riff with a smile wider than the Lake Geneva shoreline (I'm stopping to go do that right now. Be back in a minute…buh, buh, buh…buh, buh, bah da, Hell yeah! BTW, Blackmore says that everyone plays it wrong. It's an upstroke on the strings, not down). Simply put, ABBA is not rock and roll. Just stop. How about YES, not inducted until 2017! (Are you fucking for real?) Chris Squire was denied being inducted while he was alive. (Geddy was all class and played with humility and perfection during their set.) Judas Priest and Iron Maiden are not nominated but Janet Jackson is? (Hang on. My head just fell off.)

This has all led to another unfortunate situation: pitting rock aficionados against other artists who are truly phenomenal, yet not quite what the fans had in mind when such a distinction was announced; and the subsequent confusion over related accolades. I recently read an opinion piece on why Prince should be considered the greatest rock guitarist in history. I want to tread carefully here because Prince is unquestionably a once in a lifetime artist and he deserves to be in the Hall of Fame. He has made contributions across many platforms, rock included. He's got all the iconography: he's a lanky dude with stage moves, he's got skills, he even has the unique axe (a Japanese version of the H.S. Anderson (Hohner branded) Mad Cat Telecaster, which was released in 1973 by the Morris company. He bought his in 1980. I don't hold much of an opinion about those Cloud and Symbol guitars he also used.) I know many guitar fans who love this guy, as do I. I saw him at MSG right after the *Purple Rain* album and movie and the concert was incredible. The guy was a multi-faceted artist and performer. Kudos all around, but this is where I diverge. I came away from that show with all the good feelings of just having seen something incredible, but there was no feeling of just having seen the greatest guitar player of all time. I had already seen Beck, Clapton, Page, Iommi, Blackmore, Gilmour, Healey, Gallagher, Perry and Whitford, Van Halen, Marino, Lifeson…the list is pretty long, and Prince just wasn't knocking any of those guys out of the running. No disrespect to the writer of that article on Prince, but this is where the distinctions between what players and fans of the long-held impressions of what classifies a "rock" guitarist become more defined. Prince himself is quoted as saying to Guitar Player magazine in 1994, "I always wanted to be thought of as a guitarist, but you have a hit, and you know what happens next." Yes, I saw Prince jam out to "While My

Guitar Gently Weeps" alongside Tom Petty and others at the George Harrison tribute at the Rock and Roll Hall of Fame, but as good as it was, it does not leapfrog him over the countless others who have killed that solo over the past 50 years.

And yes, the intro to "When Doves Cry" catches the interest of guitar players, but can you really say that it is a better intro than…oh, let's see… "Eruption" or "Pride and Joy"? This is not about exclusivity, or leaving artists out of some secret club, it's more about honesty and respect on both sides. Music is all about diversity AND individual voices. We can't drown out the virtue of singularity in a chorus of homogeneity. If we're all the same, then none of us are different. Prince is indeed a great guitarist, but why put him under the scrutiny of labeling him "the best rock guitarist". The guy defied labels all of his life. Don't stick one on him in his passing, especially if it's going to stir division.

Horseman #4: The Duesenberg

No, not the car, the guitar (huh?). More specifically the Duesenberg - Alliance Series Johnny Depp guitar. Here's a description from their website: "What makes this guitar even more unique is the custom tapped JD-63 pickup which was specially designed to meet every characteristic of a classic open sounding single coil. Taking it a step further we offer the option of adding 1963 turns of pickup wire (1963 is Johnny's year of birth) to the signal creating a warmer and crunchier tone."

Ok, so they decided that "taking it a step further" by matching coil windings to the year of Johnny Depp's birth would give a better sound than, oh I don't know, actual science. (But can't you just feel the warmth of those birthday windings? Why hasn't Seymour Duncan figured this out? Loser.)

Signature model guitars and the suckers (sorry, intelligent consumers) who buy them belong in a class unto themselves. Put them all in a room together, lock the door and grab a Les Paul. The Les Paul is arguably the most recognizable guitar in the world and has set the standard for rock guitar construction ever since. It's a perfect recipe for solid body, set neck construction. This is the one and only signature that has mattered in the history of the solid body electric guitar since it was invented by, uh, LES PAUL! I know we've heard this story before, but apparently people need to be reminded. Who can truly claim to have had anywhere near the impact on the design and sound of an instrument as Les Paul? If it wasn't for Les Paul's ingenuity (and the extreme foresight of Ted McCarty, who was the only one with balls big enough to deal with Les), we probably wouldn't be having this conversation. Yes, the initial idea was a marketing concept. Les was a very popular artist at the time, but he brought a lot more to the table than just a popular name. The original 1952 Gibson Les Paul Gold top (with two P-90 pickups and an admittedly questionable wrap-under bridge/tailpiece) was about to start a revolution in the world of guitar music. After some tweaks, like the Tune-O-Matic bridge, and the game changing "humbuckers" (designed by Seth Lover and introduced in 1957), there was one piece left to the puzzle of the most sought-after guitar in history - the sunburst finish. Introduced on a new model called the Les Paul Standard, the sunburst was at first a failure (let's talk failure for a second: Serial number 8 3087 - the first yellow-to-red sunburst, and the second one shipped by Gibson that year, was recently sold in Nashville for $625,000. Slash owns the first one shipped - serial number 8 3096. God only knows what that one is worth now that provenance can be traced back to Slash. From failure to Holy Grail). The model was discontinued in 1961 due to concerns about being overweight (and maybe some scuffling with Les). Then in the mid-60s, the burgeoning guitar gods found the Les Paul. In 1964, Keith Richards stirred interest by playing a 1959 sunburst, and then in 1966, the shit hit the fan in the guise of Eric Clapton, the famous "Beano" album from the Bluesbreakers, and a 1960 Les Paul Standard. (This guitar was stolen shortly after Clapton finished the sessions, and Joe Bonamassa believes he has found it in the U.S.) Once the Les Paul regained status among the premier players of the time, Gibson had no choice but to reintroduce it in 1968. The rest is history.

The more innovative things have really happened over on the Fender side of the road. The tremolo system, first popularized by the Bigsby bridge - itself a redesign of a Kaufman Vibrola, (which was frustrating Merle Travis, so he asked a mechanic named Paul Bigsby to fix it), really took off when it was integrated into the Stratocaster guitar as the "Fender Synchronized Tremolo" and Jimi Hendrix got his hands on it. (Was there a Fender Stratocaster Hendrix signature model while Hendrix was alive? Nope.) Floyd Rose stepped up to the plate and really made the first worthwhile update since Fender's own tremolo in the 1950s, but still, just mods and personalization.

The only guy who can truly be said to be 100 percent responsible for his own guitar sound, design and style is Brian May. His "Red Special" is a handmade gift of complete ingenuity to the world of guitars: fireplace mantel wood (probably the first and last time oak was used in guitar construction); motorbike springs; and a freakin' knitting needle tip. He even designed the bridge with rolling saddles to return to the strings to tune after using the tremolo (come on, who was thinking that far ahead? The guy is a genius. BTW, the guy who played him in the movie really had the posture and position of the guitar down pat. It sold the movie for me as much as Rami Malek). That sound is instantly recognizable and incomparable. In a room full of a hundred guitars, you can pick that one out in a flash. And it's not even called the "Brian May", it's simply known as the Red Special (well…Burns, the British manufacturer did try to get in on the deal with a later signature model, but it is all built around Brian's design, and let's be honest, buying that is not gonna make you play or sound like him). If there was ever a signature-worthy instrument, boy is that it. There's even a book about the guitar itself. (I wonder whose birthday his coils are wound in honor of? Wait, that is a thing, right?)

Now on to Eddie Van Halen. Again, pretty much responsible for a revolution in guitar construction (or deconstruction - pickup screwed right into the body, eye hooks, chainsaw mods), but this time, not so much about brilliant engineering as it was about raw energy. Kramer and Charvel tried to capitalize on his over-the-top guitar concepts, as did Ernie Ball Music Man with a more refined build that resembled nothing of the old Frankenstrat, but ultimately Eddie resolved to his have his own brand and the EVH Wolfgang models (which are pretty good guitars) emerged but aren't redefining anything in the industry. So, "signature" guitars are really just an excuse by manufacturers to draw your eye and get a few extra bucks out of the consumer. You can't blame the artists, it's another revenue stream (and ego trip), but we may have reached the arc of absurdity with a model named for Johnny Depp (and now, let's introduce the band - Jack Sparrow on lead guitar!). The Hollywood Vampires is basically a novelty act for Johnny and a weekend gig for the Coop and Joe Perry (Joe had one of his medical emergencies on stage with them in Coney Island). The sad part is that the Duesenberg is probably a very good instrument. It looks great, but there's just no way I'm picking up a Johnny Depp guitar (with his birthday windings) and keeping a straight face.

So, what's a mother to do? Is there no salvation? Where do we go from here? (Which is the way that's clear? Keep looking for that…never mind). So, after all the hand wringing and whining, is this truly about the decline of the electric guitar or just a lament for lost youth? Well, facing mortality is a fact of life. Before his tragic passing at the age of 27, Hendrix had changed the electric guitar forever. Page was 25 when he recorded "Heartbreaker," Eddie Van Halen was 22 when he erupted (Ha! Get it? Sorry, couldn't help myself. BTW, dude has already had hip replacement surgery), so yeah, this is about getting older and clinging to the things that make us feel young, but there is a stark reality to the business end of this as well. In 2010, acoustics outsold electrics for the first time; Guitar Center had 1.6 billion in debt in 2017; Fender abandoned a public offering; Gibson went bankrupt this year. Going into a guitar store now is more like going into a candy shop (and we all know what too much sugar does to the kids). It's all about loud colors and busy shapes. I agree with a Gibson exec who complained recently about how all the higher end guitars are literally out of reach. If you want to check out a Les Paul or PRS or nicer Strat, you have to ask a salesperson (who doesn't have a fucking clue) because those instruments are behind the counter or high up on the wall. If you could feel the difference between a properly set-up Gibson and some Epiphone on a stand on the floor, you would know what it was like walking into a true guitar shop back in 1979.

Back in the day (an old man's reference if ever there was one), 48th Street in NYC was an absolute wonderland of every great instrument ever built. You could try out a new Strat in Manny's in the very spot where Hendrix and Dave Gilmour bought theirs, then walk across the street to the used guitar shop and play just about every guitar that was destined to be a vintage collector's dream. (God, I loved that shitty little shop).

163

Now, whatever you grab off the lower wall racks in Guitar Center is like a new car - it'll drop in value the minute you walk out the door. It's just business. There are more makers now than ever before, and competition is natural to the markets. Back in the day (again with this...oh, shit...hold on...my dentures fell out and I think I might need to pee), Gibson and Fender ruled the roost, Guild and Gretsch had their place, and the few odd makers filled in the rest. The Japanese makers like Yamaha and Ibanez struggled to get respect from the American market. PRS was really the first guitar maker that I saw first-hand make a real impact on what people were looking for in a quality instrument. When I saw that very first PRS show up in the window at Sam Ash in White Plains (yes, it got the window slot), I was ready to drain every drop of cash I could get my hands on to buy it (the thing that stopped me was the weird green finish. Not the first time I passed on an instrument that would eventually soar in value, but such is life. Back around 1982-ish, there was a late 50's sunburst Paul in the window on 48th selling for 10K. It was kinda beat up, and 10k was a lot, but damn...). The eventual Les Paul/Strat fatigue, the introduction of new shapes and finishes from fresh makers, and the perceived drop in quality of the classics, led to the independent boutique shops, like Suhr and Sadowsky, cranking out super high-quality instruments. All this just piled on the industry and led to where we are now — more and more manufacturers (again, thanks to inexpensive Asian-sector shops Johnny Depp Signature guitars.

Rock On.

Well…like the old porker said:

"Th-Th-The, Th-Th-The, Th-Th… That's all, folks!"

So long, and thanks for all the fish!

(Let the lawsuits begin…)

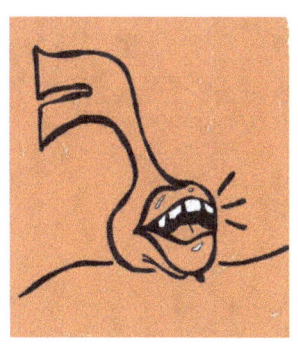